The Best
of
Isaac Watts

ANDREW MOLL

Dedicated to Isaac Otieno

May the Lord bless you and keep you

CONTENTS

1. BEHOLD THE GLORIES OF THE LAMB 4

2. HOW VAST THE TREASURE WE POSSESS......................8

3. BLESSED BE THE EVERLASTING GOD...........................12

4. ALAS! AND DID MY SAVIOUR BLEED?...........................16

5. WITH JOY WE MEDITATE THE GRACE..........................20

6. THERE IS A LAND OF PURE DELIGHT 24

7. COME, DEAREST LORD, DESCEND AND DWELL 28

8. WE ARE A GARDEN 32

9. NATURE WITH OPEN VOLUME STANDS......................36

10. COME, HOLY SPIRIT, HEAVENLY DOVE 40

11. PRAISE YE THE LORD 44

12. THE HEAVENS DECLARE YOUR GLORY, LORD.........48

13. SWEET IS THE WORK 52

14. HIGH IN THE HEAVENS 56

15. AWAKE OUR SOULS; AWAY OUR FEARS...................60

16. OUR GOD OUR HELP IN AGES PAST...........................64

17. GOD IS THE NAME MY SOUL ADORES.......................68

18. HOW BEAUTIFUL THEIR FEET 72

19. LORD, I HAVE MADE YOUR WORD MY CHOICE........76

20. FROM ALL THAT DWELL BELOW THE SKIES...........80

21. BEGIN, MY TONGUE, SOME HEAVENLY THEME........84

22. I'M NOT ASHAMED TO OWN MY LORD 88

23. MY SOUL, REPEAT HIS PRAISE 92

24. I GIVE IMMORTAL PRAISE 96

25. I'LL PRAISE MY MAKER 100

26. GIVE ME THE WINGS OF FAITH TO RISE 104

27. I SING THE ALMIGHTY POWER OF GOD 108

28. JOY TO THE WORLD...112

29. JESUS SHALL REIGN 116

30. WHEN I SURVEY THE WONDROUS CROSS...............120

ACKNOWLEDGEMENTS

Scripture quotations taken from the HOLY BIBLE,
NEW INTERNATIONAL VERSION
Copyright © 1973, 1978, 1984 by International Bible Society
Used by permission of Hodder & Stoughton,
A division of Hodder Headline Ltd.
All rights reserved.
"NIV" is a registered trademark of International Bible Society.
UK trademark number 1448790

INTRODUCTION

2019 marks the 300th anniversary of the publication of Isaac Watts' final major collection of hymns. This book marks the occasion with a personal selection of a 'top thirty' of his hymns from the 700 or so that Isaac published, mainly in three collections:

- Hymns and Spiritual Songs (1707, revised 1709);
- Divine and Moral Songs (1715);
- Psalms of David, etc. (1719).

He was a publishing phenomenon in his own time, writing not only hymns, but also books on education, reason, prayer, doctrine, astronomy and children's poetry. "Divine and Moral Songs", written primarily for children, was a best seller for two centuries, running to over a thousand editions.

His hymns are arguably his most enduring legacy. He is acknowledged as the 'father of English hymnody', and his words have touched the lives of millions of people. His greatest hits have been ever-present in hymn books for 300 years.

Much has changed in the intervening years, and I approached the task of selecting and editing Isaac's hymns with some trepidation. I expected a surfeit of archaic thought and language. I was also slightly worried that I might not find enough hymns to fill the top thirty that, 300 years on, would still speak to us today. I've ended up having to leave out some excellent ones. I have been amazed by Isaac's clarity and poetry. I have emerged from the process in awe of the master. This selection is presented from that perspective. I am not an expert in this field, simply a fan. I have presented the hymns as a kind of countdown, so that the reader builds up towards the very finest hymns at the end of the selection. I must apologise in advance if you find that you disagree with my rankings or have a favourite hymn that I've omitted.

Isaac has a message for us for today because:

- his hymns are saturated in the timeless truths of the Bible;
- he purposefully wrote with simplicity and clarity and his words are bright and sharp even now;
- at the same time his poetry is excellent, with lovely turns of phrase and deft touches of colour and humour;
- his writing reaches both our understanding and our emotions.

I have taken the following approach to editing the hymns for this selection. There are a few archaic words and verses that are generally amended or left out and I have followed this practice with reference to standard hymn books. However, without exception I have started from the originals and in a number of cases retained words and some of the verses that have been more commonly pruned or changed by hymn book compilers over the years. I have made the smallest changes to modernise an odd archaic word or phrase, and I have changed 'thy' to 'you' throughout for the purposes of using these hymns as prayers today. It has been a revelation to study the way in which he skillfully paraphrases Bible texts, never straying far from the source but finding colourful, elegant ways of shedding new light on the scripture.

So the great man speaks eloquently in the power of God's Holy Spirit. Consequently the words retain a relevance and energy to inspire us today.

The hymns are presented in this book, each with an introduction, followed by Bible excerpts that inspired them or relate to them, then the hymns themselves.

May the same Lord who inspired Isaac grant us a spirit of joy and peace and a love for Jesus, as we make his words our own in reading, reflection and prayer.

1.   BEHOLD THE GLORIES OF THE LAMB

This is where the story of Isaac's hymns begins. He had studied for four years at the Dissenting Academy at Stoke Newington in London. Now, aged about 22, he has returned home to Southampton. On Sunday he attends the service at the non-conformist Above Bar meeting-house. Afterwards Isaac discusses the service with his father. He is critical of the quality of the hymns, which would have been metrical psalm settings. His father suggests that if the hymns are not good enough perhaps Isaac should write one himself. As a result, at the evening service the congregation has a new hymn to sing. Unknown to them, this is a turning point in the history of Christian music and the beginnings of a major tradition of English hymnody.

It's a really good hymn too. It has the freshness and vigour of youth, qualities which Isaac was to maintain in his hymns even as the years passed. And it begins with a young man's confidence and enthusiasm – behold! Look up, everyone, this is something new to present to the Lord. Here is a song that's not been heard before. These are words to help us present our prayers like a beautiful fragrance to Jesus, and our praise like the celestial sound of harps. And the Lord is delighted, he loves to answer our prayers and receive our praise (verse 3).

After three verses telling us, the reader or listener, *about* God and Jesus, verses 4 to 6 are then addressed *to* God and Jesus. That shifting of the perspective is a technique that Isaac uses in a number of the hymns in this book.

So as Isaac celebrates Jesus, the Lamb of God who died for us, and his exaltation; he blesses him forever and acknowledges him as the embodiment of God's salvation, glory and joy.

The impetuousness of youth that instigated the writing of the hymn in the first place resurfaces in the final stanza. Isaac acclaims Jesus as Lord, then pleads with him to hurry up – to "shorten the delaying days" - and return in all his glory.

Isaac would return this passage in his maturity and produce a better-known hymn based on it – "Come let us join our cheerful songs" – but I rather like the rawness and vibrancy of this youthful attempt.

As Psalm 96 says:

> O sing a new song to the Lord!
> Let the whole earth sing to the Lord!
> Tell everyone about the amazing things
> he does.

Lord, may I sing your new song, a song of adoration.

When I saw him, I fell at his feet as though dead. Then he placed his right hand on me and said:

> *Do not be afraid.*
> *I am the First and the Last.*
> *I am the Living One;*
> *I was dead, and now look,*
> *I am alive for ever and ever!*
> *And I hold the keys of death and Hades.*

(Revelation 1:17-18)

A new song to the Lamb that was slain

Behold the glories of the Lamb
amidst his Father's throne;
prepare new honours for his name,
and songs before unknown.

Let elders worship at his feet,
the Church adore around,
with vials full of odours sweet,
and harps of sweetest sound.

Those are the prayers of the saints,
and these the hymns they raise:
Jesus is kind to our complaints,
he loves to hear our praise.

Eternal Father, who shall look
into your secret will?
Who but the Son should take that book,
and open every seal?

Now to the Lamb that once was slain,
be endless blessings paid;
salvation, glory, joy remain
forever on your head.

The worlds of nature and of grace
are put beneath your power.
Then shorten these delaying days,
and bring the promised hour.

2. HOW VAST THE TREASURE WE POSSESS

The second hymn in this collection takes us forward in time to 1724, and the latest hymn in this selection. A pair of hymns were appended to a volume of Isaac's sermons 1721-1724. The hymns were "How vast the treasure" and "My soul, survey thy happiness." The two hymns have generally been merged and edited to form the hymn printed below. It was written when Isaac was in his forties. In just over twenty years he had written most of his 700 or so hymns, revolutionizing English church worship in the process. All the remaining hymns in this book were published in that period.

Isaac still had many years ahead of him, which he would use productively in writing and publishing educational, devotional and non-fiction works. But this hymn is a kind of bookend, looking back, "surveying", reflecting on the lessons he had learnt from life between 22 and 45. The first half of the hymn brims with thankfulness. "How vast the treasure we possess" – here is a very contented man. Things must be going well for him – "the world is ours." His hope for the future is pretty healthy too – "and worlds to come!" here, it seems, is someone who has been blessed with peace and plenty in this life. Looking back, Isaac certainly had much to be thankful for – his exceptional talent, a purposeful life as a pastor and the satisfaction of a supremely creative period in his life; he enjoyed the support of friends, family, congregation and patrons. However, I would not want to leave the impression that Isaac led a cosily sheltered life, tucked safely away from the harsh realities.

Exactly halfway through this hymn "surveying his happiness", Isaac takes us in an unexpected direction. The clues begin with the strange verse from 1 Corinthians 3:2 that inspired the hymn: "I gave you milk, not solid food, for you were not yet ready for it. Indeed, you are still not ready."

Isaac's adult years brought several disappointments. He suffered from a debilitating illness. This became so severe in 1713 that he had to abandon his duties as a pastor. His time off lasted for 4 years. He returned to his pastoral role but was never completely free of this recurring malady. A brief encounter with romance ended in a rather unkind rejection on account of his unattractive looks. Dissenters like Isaac also remained barred from some establishment privileges and were occasionally persecuted by both the established church and the London mob.

"If bread of sorrows be my food, those sorrows work my lasting good" writes Isaac. Here we find an acceptance of limitations – there is something to be gained even from painful constraints. So please don't mistake the thankfulness that exudes from this and many of the other hymns in this selection as the smugness of a person sheltered from hardship. Far from it. It is the wisdom of a man who found a positive approach to what life throws at us. We might put it in terms of maturing through dealing with life's difficulties. We can certainly see the attraction of a thankful mindset even in adversity. Ultimately if it comes down to a choice between bitterness and thankfulness then Isaac is helping us to choose the latter.

Lord, give me a thankful heart, whatever may come.

The kingdom of heaven is like treasure hidden in a field.
When a man found it, he hid it again,
and then in his joy went and sold all he had
and bought that field.

(Matthew 13:44)

...we have this treasure in jars of clay to show that this all-
surpassing power is from God and not from us.
We are hard pressed on every side, but not crushed;
perplexed, but not in despair;
persecuted, but not abandoned;
struck down, but not destroyed.
We always carry around in our body the death of Jesus,
so that the life of Jesus may also be revealed in our body.

(2 Corinthians 4:7-10)

The Christian's treasure

How vast the treasure we possess!
How rich your bounty, king of grace!
This world is ours, and worlds to come;
earth is our lodge, and heaven our home.

All things are ours: the gifts of God;
the purchase of a Saviour's blood;
while the good Spirit shows us how
to use, and to improve them too.

If peace and plenty crown my days,
they help me, Lord, to speak your praise;
if bread of sorrows be my food,
those sorrows work my lasting good.

I would not change my blessed estate
for all the world calls good or great;
and while my faith can keep her hold,
I envy not the sinner's gold.

Father, I wait your daily will;
you shall divide my portion still;
grant me on earth what you deem best,
till death and heaven reveal the rest.

3.   BLESSED BE THE EVERLASTING GOD

The seeds of the Industrial Revolution were planted in Isaac's lifetime. Thomas Savery is generally credited with building the first steam engine in 1698. This was closely followed by the Newcomen commercial steam engine which was used to pump water. The working of this early engine was described by a contemporary as "a clumsy and apparently a very painful process, accompanied by an extraordinary amount of wheezing, sighing, creaking and bumping." However, the leap in technology brought revolutionary potential. Later in the 18th century Matthew Boulton, one of the architects of the Industrial Revolution, said to a visitor to his factory "I sell here, sir, what all the world desires to have – Power."

The Christian faith possesses a revolutionary power of its own. Peter summed it up in the first Christian sermon in Acts 2:32-33: "God has raised this Jesus to life, and we are all witnesses to the fact. Exalted to the right hand of God, he has received from the Father the promised Holy Spirit and has poured out what you now see and hear."

Peter also provided the letter (1 Peter) on which this hymn is based. Peter was, of course, an eyewitness to the resurrection of Jesus and his letter, like his sermon, places the resurrection as the pivot and the power of Christian faith and hope. Only a few of the hymns in this selection refer explicitly to Jesus' resurrection, but it is the dynamic that lies behind every single one. For instance:

- Jesus shall reign where'er the sun...because of his resurrection from the dead;

- Joy to the world....he rules the world with truth and love...as the risen Lord;
- And the love so amazing, so divine that demands my soul, my life, my all – elicits our response because it is not just about a historical act of Jesus, but a relationship with the risen, living Lord.

The "Companion to Hymns and Psalms" describes Isaac's "consummate skill" in binding words and phrases from 1 Peter into "Blessed be the everlasting God." The result is four compact verses conveying foundational truths of Christian belief and the powerful dynamic of Christian faith. It's a good idea to pause after each verse or read each verse twice to allow these thoughts to sink in.

The first verse presents facets of God's nature – his immortality, mercy, majesty, and identity as Jesus' Father. The response is to bless and praise and adore him. The second verse states two fundamental truths: firstly that Jesus, the Son of God, was raised from the dead, and secondly that this leads us to hope that we will live for ever. The phrase "lively hope" dances with excitement and energy. The third verse reflects once more on that hope, but now in terms of its permanence and solidity, as an inheritance that cannot rot away.

Finally, the hymn considers the implications of these massive claims about God, Jesus and eternal life for our lives today, here and now. Today a great power is keeping us; today we are walking by faith as strangers here; today we walk on empowered by our lively hope.

Lord, may I know the power of your risen life.

Praise be to the God and Father of our Lord Jesus Christ! In his great mercy he has given us new birth into a living hope through the resurrection of Jesus Christ from the dead, and into an inheritance that can never perish, spoil or fade.

This inheritance is kept in heaven for you, who through faith are shielded by God's power until the coming of the salvation that is ready to be revealed in the last time.

(1 Peter 1:3-5)

Hope of heaven by the resurrection of Christ

Blessed be the everlasting God,
the Father of our Lord;
be his abounding mercy praised,
his majesty adored.

When from the dead he raised his Son,
and called him to the sky,
he gave our souls a lively hope
that they should never die.

There's an inheritance divine
reserved against that day;
it's uncorrupted, undefiled,
and cannot waste away.

Saints by the power of God are kept
till the salvation come;
we walk by faith as strangers here,
till Christ shall call us home.

4. ALAS! AND DID MY SAVIOUR BLEED?

In 1850 a young woman attended a series of revival meetings at Thirtieth Street Methodist Church, New York City. On two evenings she responded to the call to go forward and kneel at the altar but did not find the peace she hoped for. The third night, 20th November, she went forward once more, and as she knelt the congregation began to sing the "grand old consecration hymn" - "Alas! And did my savior bleed?" When they reached the final lines – "here, Lord, I give myself away," her "soul was flooded with celestial light", she sprang to her feet and shouted "Hallelujah!" Her name was Fanny Crosby, and she went on to live a life of devotion, reflected in her own famous revival hymns such as "Blessed Assurance."

This very personal hymn expressing Isaac's own response to the death of Jesus on the cross has been pivotal in many other lives since. It is personal, almost a metaphysical poem, but Isaac's technique of starting it with four questions draws us also into the story. The first two questions begin "and.." creating the sense of arriving part way through the event. The trial of Jesus has taken place, as has his torture, the crown of thorns, the taunts of soldiers and onlookers, the agonizing progress to Golgotha, and the nailing to the cross.

And now we're joining the scene with Isaac as he contemplates those questions – a blood-strewn saviour? A dying king? For my sake? For my sins? The answer comes with exclamation marks! An outburst of astonishment! This is the revelation - we are witnessing divine pity, grace and love that are amazing, unknown, and beyond measure.

But the wonder is quickly consumed by horror at the deed. On the day of Jesus' crucifixion, darkness descended on the land, the sun gone into hiding, as Isaac puts it, in response to God dying at the hands of humanity. Like the sun, Isaac would like to hide his face for embarrassment at the cross, dissolve his heart and melt his eyes to nothingness. He wishes the ground could swallow him up. This is grief at the realisation of how humanity treated the Son of God when he came to his own; it is the anguish of seeing someone you have come to love enduring such agony.

Just in time Isaac lifts his head and rises above his remorse. He sees that hiding is no solution and no response. In its place comes a new determination and a new commitment to give his whole self to the God who gave himself for all.

As Fanny Crosby said, in making her commitment at the end of that hymn on 20th November 1850, "for the first time I realised that I had been trying to hold the world in one hand and the Lord in the other."

Lord, the cross - amazing love - amazing gift.

At noon, darkness came over the whole land until three in the afternoon. And at three in the afternoon Jesus cried out in a loud voice,

"Eloi, Eloi, lema sabachthani?"
(which means "My God, my God, why have you forsaken me?").

When some of those standing near heard this, they said, "Listen, he's calling Elijah." Someone ran, filled a sponge with wine vinegar, put it on a staff, and offered it to Jesus to drink. "Now leave him alone. Let's see if Elijah comes to take him down," he said.

With a loud cry, Jesus breathed his last.

The curtain of the temple was torn in two from top to bottom. And when the centurion, who stood there in front of Jesus, saw how he died, he said, "Surely this man was the Son of God!"

(Mark 15:33-39)

Godly sorrow arising from the sufferings of Christ

Alas! and did my Saviour bleed!
And did my sovereign die?
Would he devote that sacred head
for such a one as I?

Was it for crimes that I had done
he groaned upon the tree?
Amazing Pity! Grace unknown!
And love beyond degree!

Well might the sun in darkness hide,
and shut its glories in,
when God the mighty maker died
for his own creature's sin.

Thus might I hide my blushing face,
while his dear cross appears,
dissolve my heart in thankfulness,
and melt my eyes to tears.

But tears of grief cannot repay
the debt of love I owe;
here, Lord, I give myself away,
as all that I can do.

5. WITH JOY WE MEDITATE THE GRACE

In "Jesus Christ Superstar" the High Priest and his cronies feature as pantomime villains. With their black outfits and venomous hatred they hang around the story like a clutch of carrion crows. The High Priest, Caiaphas, was at the forefront of the political manouevres to ensure that Jesus died: "better for one man to die than the whole nation perish." When we use the title "High Priest", Caiaphas is probably the model etched in our minds. Even if we can put Caiaphas out of mind, we're stuck with images of ancient religious rituals and gory animal sacrifice.

This makes the opening of Isaac's hymn "With joy we meditate the grace" slightly problematic. Its subject, in line 2, is our High Priest above. Isaac is following the imagery and thought processes of the New Testament Letter to the Hebrews, difficult for us to relate to.

A way through this is to think of it in modern Human Resources terms. Start by thinking about Israel's High Priest as a post not a person. The job description for the High Priest post included:
- to act as a representative of the people before God;
- to represent God's love and judgment to the people;
- to perform that role with empathy and compassion.

It was an impossible job to get right, and many fell a long way short, lost in a minefield of politics, compromises and religion. The victims of the High Priests' shortcomings were, as always, ordinary people. When the High Priests got it wrong, they were misrepresented before God, and God's work in the world was misrepresented to them. No High Priest could ever have met that job spec. Then Jesus came along. He wasn't a High Priest but his job was to carry out a very similar role not only for the people of Israel but for all humanity. And this particular person, Jesus, matched the job role perfectly.

Isaac tells us some lovely truths about the characteristics of Jesus in this role – and how this helps us:

- You may feel that no-one understands the problems you face – but Jesus absolutely does, he stood in our shoes (verse 2).
- You may feel you have no hope of redemption – but Jesus died for you, his innocent death enabling him to become redeemer (verse 3).
- You may feel that you're on your own, and no-one cares – but Jesus feels for you, and bears your pain (verse 4).
- You may feel feeble and worthless – but you are no such thing in Jesus' eyes, he loves you with tenderness and compassion (verse 5).

The hymn concludes with one of Isaac's classic last verses. It helps us to take in the amazing grace of Jesus and to feel emboldened to approach our wonderful saviour in our need: "Then let our humble faith address his mercy and his power; we shall obtain delivering grace in the distressing hour."

Lord, so tender and full of compassion, help me in my weakness.

Therefore, since we have a great high priest who has ascended into heaven, Jesus the Son of God, let us hold firmly to the faith we profess.

For we do not have a high priest who is unable to empathize with our weaknesses, but we have one who has been tempted in every way, just as we are—yet he did not sin.

Let us then approach God's throne of grace with confidence, so that we may receive mercy and find grace to help us in our time of need.

(Hebrews 4:14-16)

Christ's compassion to the weak and tempted

With joy we meditate the grace
of our High Priest above;
his heart is made of tenderness,
and ever yearns with love.

Touched with a sympathy within,
he knows our feeble frame;
he knows what sore temptations mean,
for he has felt the same.

But spotless, innocent, and pure,
the great Redeemer stood,
while Satan's fiery darts he bore,
and did resist to blood.

He, in the days of feeble flesh,
poured out his cries and tears,
and in his measure feels afresh
what every member bears.

He'll never quench the smoking flax,
but raise it to a flame;
the bruised reed he never breaks,
nor scorns the meanest name.

Then let our humble faith address
his mercy and his power;
we shall obtain delivering grace
in the distressing hour.

6. THERE IS A LAND OF PURE DELIGHT

The young Isaac has returned to Southampton from London for a time. One day he is wandering along the shore. Across the Solent the Isle of Wight is gleaming in the sun. It is just possible that the view prompts Isaac to recall the penultimate chapter of "A Pilgrim's Progress" in which Christian views the eternal city across the river.

John Bunyan's "A Pilgrim's Progress" was published in 1678, when Isaac was 4 years old. Like Isaac's father, John Bunyan had served time in prison for the crime of nonconformism. Bunyan's masterpiece was written during a stint in Bedford Gaol. There have been countless editions since its first publication. I have two special copies of my own. One small and well-worn copy from 1902, belonged to my grandmother and dates from the time when many homes had only two books - a Bible and a "Pilgrim's Progress." The other is a children's retelling by Geraldine McCaughrean. One of the beautiful full-page illustrations by Jason Cockcroft shows us the youthful Christian and Hopeful almost at the end of their pilgrimage. They are looking across the Final River at the sight of their destination, the gleaming City of Gold.

Isaac would have been familiar with Bunyan's story, and Isaac's words could almost have been written for that moment in "A Pilgrim's Progress." However, it's more likely that the similarities are because both John Bunyan and Isaac were immersed in the words and stories of the Bible.

So Isaac's hymn, emerging in his mind as he stands by the Solent, flows at first from the descriptions of heaven in the Book of Revelation, enhanced with pastoral images of sweet fields and flowers, and spring and living green. This prompts a second Biblical association, Moses and the people of Israel and their first view of the promised land across the River Jordan. Isaac then makes the allegory in common with Bunyan: the promised land represents heaven; the river represents death, through which we pass to get there.

Isaac makes his way home from the shoreline with the makings of a very good song in his head. One thing is certain: we all reach that shoreline at some point. Isaac's hymn aligns us with the ancient roots of our faith via Moses and the people of Israel, and with all Christians on the pilgrimage of life. The promised land is gleaming in the distance.

Lord, you have brought me safe this far. Bless me in the journey that lies ahead.

Words of Moses to the people of Israel on the verge of entering the promised land:

For the Lord your God is bringing you into a good land –
a land with streams and pools of water,
with springs flowing in the valleys and hills.

(Deuteronomy 8:7)

A prospect of heaven makes death easy

There is a land of pure delight,
where saints immortal reign.
Infinite day excludes the night,
and pleasures banish pain.

There everlasting spring abides,
and never-withering flowers:
death, like a narrow sea, divides
this heavenly land from ours.

Sweet fields beyond the swelling flood
stand dressed in living green:
so to the Hebrews Canaan stood,
while Jordan rolled between.

But timorous mortals start and shrink
to cross this narrow sea,
and linger, shivering on the brink,
and fear to launch away.

Could we but make our doubts remove,
those gloomy doubts that rise,
and see the Canaan that we love
with unbeclouded eyes!

Could we but climb where Moses stood,
and view the landscape o'er,
not Jordan's stream, nor death's cold flood,
should fright us from the shore.

7. COME, DEAREST LORD, DESCEND AND DWELL

Every year at Wimbledon people queue out on the common for tickets, many camping overnight. A group of local Christians called LOVE ALL SERVE ALL take them food and drink and chat to them. One of the organisers says "We just want to help them move a step closer to understanding a God who loves them."

Ephesians 3:14-21 is one of the purple patches of Paul's letters. It is essentially a prayer cum blessing that we will move closer to understanding God's love for us in three steps: to grasp it, to know it and to be filled with it.

At the heart of the passage are some dimensions of God's love: its breadth, length, height and depth. Numerous hymn writers have picked up on this imagery:

- From Charles Wesley ("What shall I do my God to love, my loving God to praise?")
- through Victorian hymn writers ("Just as I am" and "It passeth knowledge")
- to modern choruses ("Our God is a great big God" and "Jesus' love is very wonderful")

The movements to "Jesus' love is very wonderful", with its arm actions for the height, depth and width of Jesus' love, bring out a serious point. The actions form the shape of the cross. This, I believe, is an interesting coincidence with the earliest origins of this passage, possibly in the context of a baptismal blessing. We can imagine an early Christian minister making the sign of the cross to tie in with the affirmation of the height, depth, width, breadth of God's love for the new believer. The cross is the place to look for the clearest demonstration of the extent of God's love for us and for all people.

"Come, dearest Lord" is Isaac's reflection on that marvellous passage from Ephesians. It's not so much a paraphrase as a response. Isaac grasps the wonderful love that God has for us, he knows it, he is filled with it. Here is his own heart-felt love in response. If Ephesians 3:14-21 is a kind of baptismal blessing, Isaac's hymn is for the believer to rise up from the waters and welcome Jesus into every corner of our lives. This is one of his most intimate hymns.

It's a prayer in verse 1 for Jesus to enter our hearts, a process of faith and love. The result is beyond words to tell, but involves knowing and tasting and feeling the joy of the presence of the Lord.

It's a prayer in verse 2 for our hearts and souls to be widened by receiving the love of Jesus which is higher and broader and longer and deeper than we can ever fathom – unmeasurable grace – more than enough to fill our hearts, enlarge our souls and give us robust inner strength.

It's a prayer in verse 3 of praise, honouring the God whose power exceeds anything we can understand, and whose gracious design for human beings is that we should be filled and blessed with his boundless love.

Lord, come to my heart today and fill me with your love.

For this reason I kneel before the Father,
from whom every family
in heaven and on earth derives its name.
I pray that out of his glorious riches
he may strengthen you with power
through his Spirit in your inner being,
so that Christ may dwell in your hearts through faith.

And I pray that you, being rooted and established in love,
may have power, together with all the Lord's holy people,
to grasp how wide and long and high and deep
is the love of Christ,
and to know this love that surpasses knowledge—
that you may be filled to the measure of all the fullness of
God.

Now to him who is able to do immeasurably more
than all we ask or imagine,
according to his power that is at work within us,
to him be glory in the church and in Christ Jesus
throughout all generations, for ever and ever!
Amen.

(Ephesians 3:14-21)

The love of Christ shed abroad in the heart

Come, dearest Lord, descend and dwell
by faith and love in every breast;
then shall we know, and taste, and feel
the joys that cannot be expressed.

Come, fill our hearts with inward strength,
make our enlarged souls possess,
and learn the height, and breadth, and length
of your unmeasurable grace.

Now to the God whose power can do
more than our thoughts or wishes know,
be everlasting honours done
by all the church, through Christ his Son.

8.   WE ARE A GARDEN

Here's an 18th century definition of "www": the world's wide wilderness. I think it may have brought a smile to Isaac's face to throw in a tongue twister that tangles the words like brambles underfoot in a wild wood to represent the snags and snares of our lives in this wide world. Isaac sees the "www" as a place where we lose a sense of God, purpose and order. The absence of these things can contribute to a downward spiral. Human beings come to be regarded as just another animal, and survival of the fittest can push out care and compassion.

In "We are a garden" Isaac corrects us from too low a view of the human condition. His words are drawn from Genesis and the Song of Songs. We can hear echoes of Milton's "Paradise Lost" with which Isaac was familiar. Coincidentally John Milton died in 1674, the year that Isaac was born. In book IV he describes Adam and Eve, the archetypal human beings, in the highest possible terms:

> "Two of far nobler shape erect and tall,
> God-like erect, with naked honour clad
> In naked majesty seemed lords of all,
> And worthy seemed, for in their looks divine
> The image of their glorious Maker shone." (lines 288-)

Isaac's first verse likens us to a garden planted by God, chosen, tended, made for a purpose. In verses 2 to 4, we become like trees in the garden, again tended, made for a purpose. Now God's Spirit breathes through the leaves like gusts of wind. Isaac imagines this releasing love, faith and joy, blown through the air, 'flowing abroad.' We are that garden.

This is all preparation for the crowning glory of the poem, verses 5 and 6, the visit of our Lord to his garden. Isaac compares the presence of Jesus in our lives to a feast in which we eat from the tree of life, tasting his own blessings, goodness and love. The poem ends in verse 7 with adoration, more praise than tongues can give.

We have travelled some way from the world's wide wilderness to the pinnacle of all that humanity could be: made in God's image, inspired by God's Holy Spirit, sharing the Spirit's gifts, enjoying the presence of Jesus, lost in adoration.

Lord, may I recognise your image in all the people I meet. May I delight in them as you delight in me.

You are a garden locked up, my sister, my bride;
you are a spring enclosed, a sealed fountain.
Your plants are an orchard of pomegranates
with choice fruits, with henna and nard,
nard and saffron, calamus and cinnamon,
with every kind of incense tree,
with myrrh and aloes and all the finest spices.
You are a garden fountain, a well of flowing water
streaming down from Lebanon.
Awake, north wind, and come, south wind!
Blow on my garden,
that its fragrance may spread everywhere.
Let my beloved come into his garden
and taste its choice fruits.

(Song of Songs 4:12-16)

The church the garden of Christ

We are a garden walled around,
chosen and made peculiar ground;
a little spot, enclosed by grace
out of the world's wide wilderness.

Like trees of myrrh and spice we stand,
planted by God the Father's hand;
and all his springs in Zion flow,
to make the young plantation grow.

Awake, O, heavenly wind, and come,
blow on this garden of perfume;
Spirit divine! descend and breathe
a gracious gale on plants beneath.

Make our best spices flow abroad
to entertain our Saviour God;
and faith, and love, and joy appear,
and every grace be active here.

Our Lord into his garden comes,
well pleased to smell our poor perfumes,
and calls us to a feast divine,
sweeter than honey, milk, or wine.

Eat of the tree of life, my friends,
the blessings that my Father sends;
your taste shall all my goodness prove,
and drink abundance of my love.

Jesus, we will frequent your board,
and sing the bounties of our Lord;
but the rich food on which we live
demands more praise than tongues can give.

9. NATURE WITH OPEN VOLUME STANDS

The British Library holds a first edition of "Robinson Crusoe" published in 1719. It is regarded by many as the first English novel. Its author, Daniel Defoe, was a contemporary of Isaac Watts. Like Isaac, he belonged to the dissenting tradition and grew up during its persecution in the restoration years. Defoe's readers opened their new book in 1719 and found themselves entering an exotic world. The frontispiece with its iconic pen and ink illustration sets the tone for an exotic tale of shipwreck and island castaway adventure.

Isaac's hymn "Nature with open volume stands" is built around the imagery of opening up the pages of a book:

- The first verse describes a volume open before us. The book is the created world around us. The story it tells is one of the Maker's greatness and praise. As Paul wrote in Romans 1:20: " For since the creation of the world God's invisible qualities – his eternal power and divine nature – have been clearly seen, being understood from what has been made, so that men are without excuse."
- The second verse describes an illustration, drawn in lines of crimson. It is a picture of the cross. It is this illustration that depicts most clearly the glory of God. The picture of the cross was Paul's message to the people at Corinth in 1 Corinthians 1:22: "...we preach Christ crucified... "
- In verse three Isaac directs us to three words written on the page - power, wisdom and love. Isaac has notably added a third word – love - to the message of Paul in 1 Corinthians 1:24:

"...Christ the power of God and the wisdom of God."

The title page of "Robinson Crusoe" promised "strange surprising adventures." People loved it. It sold like hot cakes, with four editions printed in its first year alone.

In "Nature with open volume stands", Isaac has used the first three verses to open up the book, show an illustration and give us the key words. The remaining three verses assess the impact of such a "book" that tells us about God in nature and on the cross. How does this volume change people's lives? The outcomes are profound. Isaac is taking us to the very heart of God and that mysterious combination of grace and judgment brought about by Jesus (verse 4). He offers us the noblest life that the spirit can know (verse 5). He invites us to hear sounds of love and worship that are beyond human comprehension but are attuned to the depths of our being (verse 6).

Isaac has opened the pages of a book before us. Through the story he has to tell we are taken on the most profound, strange and surprising adventure of faith in the God of nature and the God of the cross.

Lord, may I read your story in the world around me and in the Bible, and be inspired to love.

Jews demand signs and Greeks look for wisdom,
but we preach Christ crucified:
a stumbling block to Jews and foolishness to Gentiles,
but to those whom God has called, both Jews and Greeks,
Christ the power of God and the wisdom of God.
For the foolishness of God is wiser than human wisdom,
and the weakness of God is stronger than human strength.

(1 Corinthians 1:22-25)

Christ crucified, the wisdom and power of God

Nature with open volume stands,
to spread her Maker's praise abroad;
and every labour of his hands
shows something worthy of our God.

But in the grace that rescued man
his brightest form of glory shines;
here, on the cross, is fairest drawn,
in precious blood and crimson lines.

Here his whole name appears complete;
no wit can guess, nor reason prove,
which of the letters best is written:
the power, the wisdom, or the love.

Here I behold his inmost heart,
where grace and vengeance strangely join,
piercing his Son with sharpest smart,
to make the purchased pleasure mine.

O! the sweet wonders of that cross,
where God the Saviour loved and died.
Her noblest life my spirit draws
from his dear wounds and bleeding side.

I would for ever speak his name,
in sounds to mortal ears unknown;
with angels join to praise the Lamb,
and worship at his Father's throne.

10. COME, HOLY SPIRIT, HEAVENLY DOVE

A type of still-life painting known as 'vanitas' developed in the Dutch school of the 17th century. Such paintings featured symbolic (sometimes macabre) reminders of human mortality alongside objects regarded as 'vanities', representing the fleeting pleasures of this life. A painting by Edward Collier, now in Tate Britain, uses this style to great effect, setting musical instruments, wine and jewels alongside a skull, an hour-glass, a poem on mortality and a quotation from Ecclesiastes: "Vanity of vanities, all is vanity."

It is, of course, ironic that an enduring and beautiful work of art has been created on the subject of the transitory nature of life. The faith that lay behind these paintings recognized not only the poignant beauty and delights of life but also a deeper longing within us for a greater truth, knowledge and beauty.

At the heart of this hymn, Isaac repeats the phrase 'In vain...in vain'. It is a kind of vanitas. It accentuates the distinction between the mundane, which dominates our lives, and the deeper desire for the eternal, which we so often neglect.

Isaac uses three compelling images in verses 2,3 and 4:
- 'Trifling toys' cause us to grovel through our life on earth. This in turn prevents our souls from 'flying' with eternal joys. As a modern worship song puts it "Why do you crawl when you know how to fly?" Insignificant things distract us.
- Then there is a picture of people at worship. But the atmosphere is stagnant, deadened by

formality. We hear the 'hosanna' of the song languish.

- Most dramatically, a death-bed scene follows, symbolising the faintness and coldness of our love for God.

'Trifling toys', lifeless worship, and a death-bed scene are as bleak a portrayal of our situation as the symbols in those vanitas paintings.

The bookends to the hymn, the first and last verse, repeat a prayer for God's help to quicken our deadness and warm the coldness of our hearts. We need God's Holy Spirit to work within us to redeem our situation and kindle new life. The inspiration is a deep appreciation of the love of Jesus for us.

Charles Wesley, who met Isaac at least once, was clearly inspired by Isaac's language in this hymn. He borrowed its imagery as the basis of one of his own finest hymns:

O thou who camest from above
The pure, celestial fire to impart,
Kindle a flame of sacred love
On the mean altar of my heart.

Lord, send your Holy Spirit to set my heart ablaze with your love.

For this reason I remind you to fan into flame the gift of God, which is in you through the laying on of my hands. For the Spirit God gave us does not make us timid, but gives us power, love and self-discipline.

So do not be ashamed of the testimony about our Lord or of me his prisoner. Rather, join with me in suffering for the gospel, by the power of God.

He has saved us and called us to a holy life— not because of anything we have done but because of his own purpose and grace. This grace was given us in Christ Jesus before the beginning of time, but it has now been revealed through the appearing of our Saviour, Christ Jesus, who has destroyed death and has brought life and immortality to light through the gospel.

(2 Timothy 1:6-10)

Breathing after the Holy Spirit;
or, fervency of devotion desired

Come, Holy Spirit, heavenly dove,
with all your quickening powers;
kindle a flame of sacred love
in these cold hearts of ours.

Look how we grovel here below,
fond of these trifling toys;
our souls can neither fly nor go
to reach eternal joys.

In vain we tune our formal songs,
in vain we strive to rise;
hosannas languish on our tongues,
and our devotion dies.

Dear Lord! and shall we ever lie
in this poor dying state?
our love so faint, so cold to you,
and yours to us so great?

Come, Holy Spirit, heavenly dove,
with all your quickening powers
come, shed abroad the Saviour's love,
and that shall kindle ours.

11. PRAISE YE THE LORD

Long before sing-a-thons and hymn marathons, the people of the 17th century demonstrated great endurance in their acts of worship. Hymns, prayers and sermons were much longer than we are used to today. During the persecution of nonconformists in the restoration era, a government spy reported on a meeting house in Yarmouth. The morning meeting was from 5 or 6 until 10, and a second service from 11 to 3. The spy counted more than 400 people in and out of the building. Even spying required the patience of a saint!

Here's the longest hymn in this book. Unlike most hymn-books, which generally omit at least verses 2 and 4, I've included all eight of the original verses. The most common tune, "Justification", stretches it out even more by repeating the last line of every verse. Isaac actually printed a PAUSE after verse 4, perhaps so that everyone could catch their breath at the halfway mark.

One of the reasons for including the full text is that it shows how Isaac keeps very close to the meaning and order of the psalm, leaving out nothing in making his paraphrase.

We can also observe the moments where Isaac applies the lens of Christian faith to the Hebrew psalm.

- In verse 2 the gathering of exiles of Israel becomes a gathering of the nations.
- In the final verse those who fear the Lord are given a contemporary Christian title, "saints."

- We also see Isaac taking some poetic licence to exaggerate the fate of the humble and the wicked. Where the psalm says humble will be sustained and the wicked cast to the ground, Isaac moves it on a level to crown the meek, reward the just and tread the wicked into the dust.

If that reads rather uncomfortably today, Isaac's final enhancement of the psalm is one of his finest lines: "He looks and loves his image there."

Those words are not in the psalm, but they represent Isaac's interpretation of the Lord's delight in his people. The Lord is truly mighty in power, shown as he calls out the stars by name and puts the clouds in the sky. But alongside that mighty power is great love for people, shown as he binds the wounds of the broken-hearted, sustains the humble and delights in those who hope in him. He really does look and love his image there.

Lord, fill my heart with praise at the thought of your greatness and goodness.

Praise the Lord. How good it is to sing praises to our God, how pleasant and fitting to praise him!

The Lord builds up Jerusalem; he gathers the exiles of Israel.

He heals the broken-hearted and binds up their wounds.

He determines the number of the stars and calls them each by name.

Great is our Lord and mighty in power; his understanding has no limit.

The Lord sustains the humble but casts the wicked to the ground.

Sing to the Lord with grateful praise; make music to our God on the harp.

He covers the sky with clouds; he supplies the earth with rain and makes grass grow on the hills.

He provides food for the cattle and for the young ravens when they call.

His pleasure is not in the strength of the horse, nor his delight in the legs of the warrior; the Lord delights in those who fear him, who put their hope in his unfailing love.

(Psalm 147:1-11)

The Divine nature, providence, and grace.

Praise ye the Lord; 'tis good to raise
our hearts and voices in his praise;
his nature and his works invite
to make this duty our delight.

The Lord builds up Jerusalem,
and gathers nations to his name;
his mercy melts the stubborn soul,
and makes the broken spirit whole.

He formed the stars, those heavenly flames;
he counts their numbers, calls their names;
his wisdom's vast, and knows no bound,
a deep where all our thoughts are drowned.

Great is our Lord, and great his might;
and all his glories infinite:
he crowns the meek, rewards the just,
and treads the wicked to the dust.

Sing to the Lord, exalt him high,
who spreads his clouds all round the sky;
there he prepares the fruitful rain,
nor lets the drops descend in vain.

He makes the grass the hills adorn,
and clothes the smiling fields with corn;
the beasts with food his hands supply,
and the young ravens when they cry.

What is the creature's skill or force,
the sprightly man, the warlike horse,
the nimble wit, the active limb?
all are too mean delights for him.

But saints are lovely in his sight,
he views his children with delight;
he sees their hope, he knows their fear,
and looks, and loves his image there.

12. THE HEAVENS DECLARE YOUR GLORY, LORD

At some point in the 1720s Isaac was looking for an introduction to astronomy, perhaps in connection with his educational responsibilities to the Abney family. It is said that, unable to find an appropriate volume, he decided to write one himself. It was published in 1726 with the title: "The knowledge of the heavens and the earth made easy, OR the first principles of geography and astronomy."

In line with Sir Isaac Newton's dictum, the book avoids mixing science and theology. (Newton wrote prolifically but separately on both). However, Isaac also wrote to a mutual friend of Newton's: "Without commencing some acquaintance with these mathematical sciences, I could never arrive at so clear a conception of many things delivered in the scriptures; nor could I raise my ideas of God the Creator to so high a pitch." (A sentiment of which Newton himself would have approved.)

Isaac holds a high and reverent view of God's work and nature revealed in the created universe and the natural world. In this hymn, which springs from Psalm 19, the heavens declare the Lord's glory, wisdom and power. Isaac's poetry shows his delight in the grandeur and order of every star, the sun in its course, the providence of night and day, the seasons, and the beauty of the changing light. This is both reinforced and deepened by the revelation of God in the Bible. God's nature is revealed in wisdom and power, but also justice and grace.

In the second verse, Isaac pictures the sun, moon and stars constantly revolving around the earth (as we perceive them), conveying God's praise. Isaac compares this to God's truth circling the world, the good news and blessing of Jesus touching every nation. This is portrayed with dynamic energy, it is unresting, a race running around the world.

In this beautifully constructed hymn, Isaac then specifically identifies Jesus with the sun. The lines "Great Sun of Righteousness, arise, bless the dark world with heavenly light" would later be taken by Charles Wesley and blended into one of his finest hymns, "Christ whose glory fills the skies." Returning to the language of Psalm 19, Isaac displays the glory of the Lord now grounded in the simple becoming wise, souls renewed, sins forgiven and hopes of heaven. These transformations of the human heart and human lives, restoring the precious image of God in people, are seen to be the noblest wonders of all the Lord's great works.

Lord, may I be aware of your glory in the world around me and in your renewal of my own being.

The heavens declare the glory of God; the skies proclaim the work of his hands. Day after day they pour forth speech; night after night they reveal knowledge.

They have no speech, they use no words; no sound is heard from them. Yet their voice goes out into all the earth, their words to the ends of the world.

In the heavens God has pitched a tent for the sun. It is like a bridegroom coming out of his chamber, like a champion rejoicing to run his course. It rises at one end of the heavens and makes its circuit to the other; nothing is deprived of its warmth.

The law of the Lord is perfect, refreshing the soul.

The statutes of the Lord are trustworthy, making wise the simple.

The precepts of the Lord are right, giving joy to the heart.

The commands of the Lord are radiant, giving light to the eyes.

The fear of the Lord is pure, enduring forever.

The decrees of the Lord are firm, and all of them are righteous.

They are more precious than gold, than much pure gold; they are sweeter than honey, than honey from the honeycomb. By them your servant is warned; in keeping them there is great reward.

But who can discern their own errors? Forgive my hidden faults. Keep your servant also from wilful sins; may they not rule over me. Then I will be blameless, innocent of great transgression.

May these words of my mouth and this meditation of my heart be pleasing in your sight, Lord, my Rock and my Redeemer.

(Psalm 19)

The books of nature and of Scripture compared

The heavens declare your glory, Lord,
in every star your wisdom shines,
but when our eyes behold your word,
we read your name in fairer lines.
The rolling sun, the changing light,
and nights and days, your power confess,
but the blessed volume you have written
reveals your justice and your grace.

Sun, moon, and stars convey your praise
round the whole earth, and never stand:
so when your truth began its race,
it touched and glanced on every land.
Nor shall your spreading gospel rest
till through the world your truth has run,
till Christ has all the nations blessed
that see the light or feel the sun.

Great Sun of Righteousness, arise,
bless the dark world with heavenly light;
your gospel makes the simple wise,
your laws are pure, your judgments right,
your noblest wonders here we view
in souls renewed and sins forgiven;
Lord, cleanse my sins, my soul renew,
and make your word my guide to heaven.

13. SWEET IS THE WORK

I'm not sure when the balance tipped between Sunday as a Holy Day and a holiday. Both are good, of course, and in the 24/7/365 western world the pattern of a special day for rest and leisure (and even worship) persists. In the Hebrew calendar (and accordingly the Christian calendar) it is the first day of the week, and the day of Jesus' resurrection. Early on, Christianity took over some of the features of the Jewish Sabbath (which is Saturday) and applied them to Sunday as a holy day. You can see the weekend emerging on the horizon.

The Old Testament scholar Walter Brueggemann has written about Sabbath as resistance. This is a reminder that the concept of a holy day has been in many times and places a cause of tension and rebellion against the powers that be. Isaac was perhaps more familiar with Sunday as an established (and sometimes enforced) day of rest for the whole community.

That was the kind of Sunday that many of us grew up with in the 1960s and 1970s. Work stopped; shops were shut; and the days seemed to pass very slowly. For some people this made Sundays constrained and interminably dull. I was greatly blessed with a very different experience. In our Methodist family, Sundays brought the family together for meals and games, sometimes complemented by a visiting preacher for lunch or tea. The day's schedule was built around two church services, the worship special, pivotal to the life of my family. At their very best, those Sundays left an impression of the world stopping and allowing harmony, tranquillity and sacredness room to flourish.

"Sweet is the work," says Isaac, "sweet is the day of sacred rest." The psalm he's working on is entitled "for the sabbath day." His thinking starts with a good Sunday in his world, but it opens up to explore the heart of worship:

- Verses 1 and 2 begin "sweet is the..." and enumerate some of the components of an act of worship - praise, thanksgiving, singing, and quietness – but most crucially the right attitude – a heart in tune with King David's, the author of many of the Bible's praise songs in the Psalms.
- With that positioning of the heart the song bursts into life in verse 3, a heart triumphing in the Lord and blessing God for his works and words and wisdom.
- Verses 4 and 5 both begin "Then I shall..." These are the outcomes of worship: a heart refined by grace; joy poured out like an anointing of oil; and a glimpse into the world of Heaven.

Graham Kendrick released a new song in 2018, "Praise him moon and stars." The first verse is taken straight from Isaac's "Sweet is the work." It's a fantastic song, and the online video shows the band, singers and audience thoroughly enjoying themselves worshipping God. Sweet is the work. In the 21st century our experience of Sundays may be quite different to that of Isaac, but the place he leads us to is as crucial today as ever – the worship of the Lord is a wonderful thing. In the words of the Shorter Westminster Catechism, question number 1, the answer is: "Our chief end is to glorify God, and to enjoy him forever."

Lord, may my heart be tuned to sing your praise.

It is good to praise the Lord and make music to your name,
O Most High, proclaiming your love in the morning
and your faithfulness at night,
to the music of the ten-stringed lyre and the melody of the
harp.
For you make me glad by your deeds, Lord;
I sing for joy at what your hands have done.
How great are your works, Lord, how profound your
thoughts!

Senseless people do not know, fools do not understand,
that though the wicked spring up like grass
and all evildoers flourish,
they will be destroyed forever.
But you, Lord, are forever exalted.
For surely your enemies, Lord, surely your enemies will
perish; all evildoers will be scattered.

You have exalted my horn like that of a wild ox;
fine oils have been poured on me.
 My eyes have seen the defeat of my adversaries;
my ears have heard the rout of my wicked foes.
The righteous will flourish like a palm tree,
 they will grow like a cedar of Lebanon;
planted in the house of the Lord,
they will flourish in the courts of our God.
They will still bear fruit in old age, they will stay fresh and
green, proclaiming,
 "The Lord is upright; he is my Rock,
and there is no wickedness in him."

(Psalm 92)

A psalm for the Lord's day

Sweet is the work, my God, my King,
to praise your name, give thanks and sing,
to show your love by morning light,
and talk of all your truth at night.

Sweet is the day of sacred rest,
no mortal cares shall seize my breast;
O may my heart in tune be found,
like David's harp of solemn sound!

My heart shall triumph in my Lord,
and bless his works, and bless his word;
your works of grace, how bright they shine!
How deep your counsels! how divine!

Then I shall share a glorious part
when grace has well refined my heart;
and fresh supplies of joy are shed,
like holy oil, to cheer my head.

Then I shall see, and hear, and know
all I desired or wished below;
and every power find sweet employ
in that eternal world of joy.

14. HIGH IN THE HEAVENS

Landscape painting did not surface as an independent genre in western art until the 17th century. It was the Dutch, enjoying their Golden Age, who gave it the name, *landschap*. Paintings without people were enjoyed for their intrinsic beauty, but there were also deeper meanings through the symbolism of the works. A leading exponent was Jacob von Ruisdael. Some of his forest scenes with tangled branches are understood to represent the darkness and confusion of humanity while at the same time affirming hope and beauty.

Landscape as a form found its way into poetry too. John Milton is credited with the first poem to be categorised as landscape – "L'Allegro" in 1632. Isaac, too, was not averse to painting landscape imagery into his hymns, symbolic of deeper meaning.

This is the landscape that he builds up in "High in the Heavens." The sun is breaking through a sky littered with dark clouds. Its beams light on a mountainous scene bordering the sea, with the ocean extending to the distant horizon. The foothills and meadows are populated with all manner of creatures. In the foreground a river runs by a mansion where a feast is prepared. In front of the house, at the centre of this picture is a glistening fountain, sparkling in the sunlight.

Isaac attaches a meaning to each component in this picture:
- The sun represents the glory of the eternal God
- The clouds are what hide or hinder God's purposes

- The mountains stand firm like God's justice
- The sea represents the depths of God's judgments
- The house is a place of refuge, God's protection
- The feast represents our salvation
- The river flows with mercy
- The fountain stands for the life that springs from God's presence
- And the light, which starts and ends the hymn, enables us to see the glory promised in the Bible

Not only does Isaac want us to appreciate the scene, he also wants us to participate in it. He invites us to step into the landscape, join in with the feast, and drink from the fountain of life.

Lord, thank you for the work of your hands in my life and in the world around me.

Your love, Lord, reaches to the heavens,
your faithfulness to the skies.
Your righteousness is like the highest mountains,
your justice like the great deep.
You, Lord, preserve both people and animals.
How priceless is your unfailing love, O God!
People take refuge in the shadow of your wings.
They feast on the abundance of your house;
you give them drink from your river of delights.
For with you is the fountain of life;
in your light we see light.

(Psalm 36: 5-9)

The perfections and providence of God

High in the heavens, eternal God,
your goodness in full glory shines,
your truth shall break through every cloud
that veils and darkens your designs;
for ever firm your justice stands,
as mountains their foundations keep;
wise are the wonders of your hands;
your judgments are a mighty deep.

Your providence is kind and large,
all living things your bounty share;
the whole creation is your charge,
but people know your special care.
My God! how excellent your grace,
from which our hope and comfort springs!
Children of Adam in distress
fly to the shadow of your wings.

From the provisions of your house
we shall be fed with sweet repast;
there mercy like a river flows,
and brings salvation to our taste;
life, like a fountain rich and free,
springs from the presence of the Lord;
and in your light our souls shall see
the glories promised in your word.

15. AWAKE OUR SOULS; AWAY OUR FEARS

Isaac Watts and Georg Frederick Handel were contemporaries, outstanding in their own particular fields. It is entirely possible that they met. We can presume that Isaac was familiar with Handel's music in some form, and would have enjoyed its elegance, exuberance and spirituality. This is especially so with the oratorios. These brought stories from the Bible to life in crowded theatres and churches, to the accompaniment of popular music of the highest order. Handel's greatest hits include "Israel in Egypt", "Solomon", "Samson", "Jephtha", "Esther" and, of course, "Messiah."

A collaboration between Watts (lyrics) and Handel (music) is a tantalising thought, but never happened. That combination would have been the Tim Rice and Andrew Lloyd-Webber of the 18th century. We do not know if their paths crossed in life, but in death both were immediately honoured in Westminster Abbey. Shortly after his death in 1748 a memorial to Isaac was completed in the Abbey, although his tomb is in the non-conformist cemetery of Bunhill Fields. His memorial in the abbey was joined by a similar one honouring Handel 11 years later, this time along with a funeral, full state honours, and burial in the Abbey.

There are several examples of the combining of Isaac's words and Handel's music, largely due to later enterprising church musicians and hymn-book editors. These people took some of Isaac's hymns and fitted them to some of Handel's greatest hits. "Awake, our souls" is a case in point, with the tune having been plucked from 1742's "Samson" thirty or more years after the words were published. The combination is a good one. The tune is energetic, with rising uplifting patterns that match the energy and upward movement of Isaac's words. One of Handel's favourite styles, by the way, was the Courante, a form which was described at the time as "chiefly characterized by the passion or mood of sweet expectation. For there is something heartfelt, something longing and also gratifying, in this melody: clearly music on which hopes are built." While the music to "Awake my soul" is not a courante, the definition equally applies.

Isaac was not blessed with robust health, and often grew tired and weary. He may not have been equipped to run a marathon, but he poured his energy, heart and soul, into his vocation, and faithful living. Life is like pressing on with a journey along a difficult road; or a race to heaven; or soaring into the sky like an eagle. These are metaphors. The courage, refreshment, hope and strength to keep on, whatever the physical circumstances of life, are real. And the source of this reality is revealed in an insightful phrase at the heart of the song - God's enduring, matchless power is ever new and ever young. Sydney Carter picked up on that phrase and adapted it in his own 20th century energetic journeying song, "One more step." But the image that stays with me from this hymn is the penultimate line, which is one of Isaac's deft personal touches, not in the original Bible passage: "On wings of love our souls shall fly." The wings, the upward motion, the energy powering Isaac's faith is his *love* for his God and his God's *love* for him.

Lord, you raise me up on wings like eagles'. Give me the strength I need for my journey.

Do you not know? Have you not heard?
The Lord is the everlasting God,
the Creator of the ends of the earth.
He will not grow tired or weary,
and his understanding no one can fathom.
He gives strength to the weary
and increases the power of the weak.
Even youths grow tired and weary,
and young men stumble and fall;
but those who hope in the Lord will renew their strength.
They will soar on wings like eagles;
they will run and not grow weary,
they will walk and not be faint.

(Isaiah. 40:28-31)

The Christian race

Awake, our souls; away, our fears,
let every trembling thought be gone;
awake, and run the heavenly race,
and put a cheerful courage on.

It is a narrow, thorny road,
and mortal spirits tire and faint;
but they forget the mighty God,
who feeds the strength of every saint.

Almighty God! whose matchless power
is ever new and ever young,
and firm endures, while endless years
their everlasting circles run.

From you, the overflowing spring,
our souls shall drink a fresh supply;
if we should trust our native strength
we melt away, and droop, and die.

Swift as an eagle cuts the air,
we'll soar on high to your abode,
on wings of love our souls shall fly,
not tiring on the heavenly road.

16. OUR GOD OUR HELP IN AGES PAST

It has become the Remembrance Sunday Hymn. Its themes of protection and consolation are appropriate for the day, as is the verse that pictures time bearing all her sons away. This evokes for us poignant images: young men, packed on station platforms about to set off for the Western Front; names on war memorials; row upon row of Portland limestone crosses. "Our God, our help in ages past" was sung at Gladstone's funeral, and has been described as a second national anthem. Isaac wrote the words around the time of the death of Queen Anne (1714), which was a time of national mourning and a constitutional crisis that threatened to cause unwelcome upheaval.

The hymn is more than just a national institution for solemn occasions and times of crisis. Experts regard it as one of the finest hymns ever written. J.R.Watson compares it to a piece of furniture made by a master, the lines perfectly shaped and jointed. Each verse slides into place like a well-made drawer in a cabinet, he says. Ian Bradley quotes a Victorian survey of Oxford professors which unanimously awarded it the accolade of the greatest of hymns. More important than all of this, it deals with universal themes and has proved a hymn of enormous help to individuals, especially when life feels out of control. It affirms God's eternal care and protection.

In the first two verses Isaac lists seven words and images about us and God. These are like the faces of a diamond, showing facets of God's protecting care for us: our help, our hope, our shelter, our home, our defence, God's throne (to shelter us), and God's arm (his strength to care for us).

Then Isaac starts stretching our perspectives. He takes us, in our imaginations, to time before the foundation of the earth. Then we race through time into an everlasting future ahead. He gives us God's perspective on a thousand ages, passing like an evening. Then he places our human life in the context of the scale of time and the universe - as fleeting as a dream that disappears on waking. But in the final verse, Isaac re-affirms that our God, who has been our help in the past, is our hope for the future.

The last verse concludes with a prayer that God will guard us through troubles until we come to him as our eternal home. We might have expected Isaac to say that God *provides us* with an eternal home, but the language is more remarkable than that. God *is* our eternal home. This hymn's marvellous lines, that stretched our perspectives of time and space, might have led us to think of our lives as insignificant, and made God seem distant and far beyond our reach. But Isaac's final, crowning conclusion is that God's relationship with us is so close we can talk of living with him and in him, as our home. O Lord, you have been our dwelling place throughout all generations.

Lord, although you are so much greater than the universe you have made, you have a place for me in your heart. With your help I can cope with the things that are beyond my control.

Lord, you have been our dwelling place
throughout all generations.
Before the mountains were born
or you brought forth the whole world,
from everlasting to everlasting you are God.
You turn people back to dust, saying,
"Return to dust, you mortals."
A thousand years in your sight are like a day that has just
gone by, or like a watch in the night.
Yet you sweep people away in the sleep of death—
they are like the new grass of the morning:
in the morning it springs up new,
but by evening it is dry and withered.

(Psalm 90:1-6)

Man frail, and God eternal

Our God, our help in ages past,
our hope for years to come,
our shelter from the stormy blast,
and our eternal home.

Under the shadow of your throne
your saints have dwelt secure;
sufficient is your arm alone,
and our defence is sure.

Before the hills in order stood,
or earth received her frame,
from everlasting you are God,
to endless years the same.

A thousand ages in your sight
are like an evening gone;
short as the watch that ends the night
before the rising sun.

Time, like an ever-rolling stream,
bears all its sons away;
they fly, forgotten, as a dream
dies at the opening day.

Our God, our help in ages past,
our hope for years to come,
O be our guard while troubles last,
and our eternal home.

17. GOD IS THE NAME MY SOUL ADORES

This hymn is a beautiful, reverent, poetic description of the transcendent majesty of God. How little we grasp of that massive reality of God! The philosopher Plato concocted an allegory of people imprisoned in a cave from birth. They sat chained, facing a wall. A fire burned some way outside the entrance to the cave so that whenever an object or creature passed by, its shadow was cast upon the wall. Those people satisfied themselves that what they could see on the cave wall was the full extent of reality. They had no concept that their cave opened out onto something much, much bigger just over their shoulders.

It may be that this famous picture of the cave is drifting through Isaac's thoughts as he ponders the infinite 'unknowability' of God. Our perception of reality is so narrow. Our encounters with even the most awesome aspects of creation leave us a long way short of grasping the nature of the creator. As a youngster, Isaac would undoubtedly have stood on the shore at Southampton watching the ocean, listening to the breakers' roar. That experience can remind us of our smallness in the scheme of things, but does not reveal to us the creator of the seas. In Isaac's time, human understanding of the scale of the universe was expanding dramatically. But understanding the vastness and mystery of space brings us only a small way towards understanding the creator.

Isaac begins to consider the enormous gap between our lives and the nature of God. It results in a sequence of opposites. We are timeboxed in a life, on a planet, in a universe, and all is constantly changing, growing, dying, regenerating, moving on. God by comparison is unchanging and eternal, outside the cycle of change and decay, life and death. Isaac gives a panoramic view of our big realities: the seas, the stars, life on earth. But they are no more than shadows on the cave wall. The God who made them and sustains them exists in a way far beyond our comprehension. Isaac concludes that if God is like a blazing light or a consuming flame, it's inconceivable that human beings could look on this light or approach such a blaze.

For Plato, it is philosophy that breaks chains, turns people round and liberates them from the limitations of the senses. Isaac offers a different perspective. As he draws towards the close of this hymn, he seems stuck with intractable questions. Given the enormous gulf between ourselves and the creator, how can we contemplate praising, seeing or approaching God? The final two lines, far from giving an answer, seem to accept that there is no solution to the problem. Only God has the wisdom to comprehend his own power, only God has the words to describe his own nature.

But there are two observations which rescue us from awed helplessness. Firstly, the hymn is not *about* God, it is a conversation with him, which acts as a counterbalance to the subject matter – Isaac is still engaged in approaching the creator personally however overwhelmingly different he is. Secondly, the hymn is not about philosophical thought, it's about adoration. My soul adores the eternal one.

Lord, may I never underestimate your awesome majesty, or your unshakeable love for me. I adore you.

So we fix our eyes
not on what is seen,
but on what is unseen,
since what is seen is temporary,
but what is unseen is eternal.

(2 Corinthians 4:18)

The Creator and Creatures

God is the name my soul adores,
almighty three, eternal one!
Nature and grace, with all their powers
Confess the infinite unknown.

Your voice produced the sea and spheres,
called stars to shine, and waves to roar;
but nothing like yourself appears
through all these spacious works of yours.

Still restless nature dies and grows;
from change to change the creatures run;
your being no succession knows,
and all your vast designs are one.

How then could humble mortals dare
to sing your glory or your grace?
Beneath your feet we lie so far,
and see but shadows of your face!

Who can behold this blazing light?
Who can approach consuming flame?
Only your wisdom knows your might,
only your word can speak your name.

18. HOW BEAUTIFUL THEIR FEET

On 10th November 1989 the world awoke to unexpected news from excited reporters and presenters: "A historic moment. The Berlin Wall can no longer contain the East German people." The UK's Prime Minister, Margaret Thatcher, announced "a great day for freedom. You can see the joy on people's faces and what freedom means to them; it makes you realise that you cannot stifle or suppress people's desire for liberty and so I watched with the same joy as everyone else."

One of Isaac's poetic techniques is the use of different characters and perspectives within his hymns. In "how beautiful their feet" he offers four perspectives on the joy of liberation. He begins, in the first two verses, by focusing on the **messengers** who, in the original context, have arrived excited and breathless with news of return from exile in Babylon. Like the reporters from Berlin they have good news, possibly unexpected news, to share. They come from the ancient prophecy of Isaiah, who pictured the day when the news would break that the exiled people of Israel are being released to return home from Babylon to Jerusalem. Isaac has a little fun, by the way, in this hymn by referencing different body parts in every verse. Here it's the beautiful feet, chattering tongues and voices of the messengers as they reach Jerusalem with the news of salvation and peace.

In verses 3 and 4, the perspective changes, rolling the clock forward from ancient prophecy and history to **our lives**, here and now. It's our ears that are happy and our eyes blessed because that message of liberation is actually a message for us. This gives us pause for thought. Because of Jesus we enjoy the privilege of peace and salvation that even the greatest figures of the Bible longed for but never fully found.

Verse 5 takes us back to the original scene and the walls of ancient Jerusalem, where **watchmen** are on guard. When they hear the news the messengers bring, they raise their voices in 'tuneful notes', waking the city with the message.

The last verse is about the root cause of this exciting news rippling through Jerusalem and our own lives. It's about **God**. He is "baring his arm", to use a biblical phrase. We might say, more colloquially, "rolling up his sleeves and getting it sorted." Our God reigns. He is the Lord of history. His hand may be seen at work in the fall of the Berlin Wall, the return of ancient Jewish exiles to Jerusalem, and the liberation he brings to our own lives.

Isaac calls this hymn "The blessedness of gospel times." In the latter part of Isaac's life, God's Spirit was clearly at work in revival. Isaac's own hymns proved an instrument of that revival, well used by the likes of Jonathan Edwards, George Whitefield and John Wesley. Hearts were moved and people in both America and Great Britain found new life in Jesus.

Lord, thank you for good news, and thank you for the peace and salvation I find in you.

How beautiful on the mountains are the feet of those who bring good news, who proclaim peace, who bring good tidings, who proclaim salvation, who say to Zion, "Your God reigns!"

Listen! Your watchmen lift up their voices; together they shout for joy. When the Lord returns to Zion, they will see it with their own eyes.

Burst into songs of joy together, you ruins of Jerusalem, for the Lord has comforted his people, he has redeemed Jerusalem. The Lord will lay bare his holy arm in the sight of all the nations, And all the ends of the earth will see the salvation of our God.

(Isaiah 52:7-10)

But blessed are your eyes because they see, and your ears because they hear. For truly I tell you, many prophets and righteous people longed to see what you see but did not see it, and to hear what you hear but did not hear it.

(words of Jesus from Matthew 13:16-17)

The blessedness of gospel times

How beautiful their feet
who stand on Zion's hill,
who bring salvation on their tongues,
and words of peace reveal.

How charming is their voice,
how sweet the tidings are:
"Zion, behold your saviour king;
he reigns and triumphs here."

How happy are our ears
that hear this joyful sound,
which kings and prophets waited for,
and sought, but never found.

How blessed are our eyes
that see this heavenly light.
Prophets and kings desired it long,
but died without the sight.

The watchmen join their voice,
and tuneful notes employ;
Jerusalem breaks forth in songs,
and deserts learn the joy.

The Lord makes bare his arm
through all the earth abroad;
let every nation now behold
their saviour and their God.

19. LORD, I HAVE MADE YOUR WORD MY CHOICE

Some people may have an impression of the Bible as a dull, sombre, sometimes incomprehensible ancient text. They may regard it as irrelevant to modern life. But to those who know and love the Bible it is a treasure trove of wisdom and beauty, and the best place to find the meaning of life and the key to salvation.

The American theologian John Piper compares his relationship with the Bible to standing by a window in a chalet overlooking the Alps. "I have stood in front of this window all these years, not to protect it from being broken, or because the owner of the chalet told me to, but because of the glory of the Alps on the other side."[1] His book, "A Peculiar Glory" goes on to describe the lifelong blessing he has known of "being held on to by beauty, that is the glory of God" revealed in the scripture.

In "Lord I have your word my choice", Isaac paints a picture of the Bible which is very similar to John Piper's view from the window. His words are a poetic expansion of Psalm 119:111: "Your statutes are my heritage forever; they are the joy of my heart."

Isaac is just as excited as John Piper about the glory of God to be found in the scripture.

- In verse 1, the Bible causes Isaac's "noblest powers" to rejoice and engages his "warmest thoughts";

---

[1] Piper, John *A Peculiar Glory*, London:Inter-Varsity Press, 2016, p.11

- In verse 2, he describes its stories, laws and promises as a source of "ever fresh delight";
- Verse 3 pictures the Bible as a panoramic landscape with unknown wealth, springs of life, seeds of bliss, and (like Piper) hidden glory;
- Verse 4 grounds this hymn in the deepest realities of life. The Bible comes into its own when we face difficulties, sorrows or bereavement. Its words give us comfort and peace, and an assurance of God's love and purpose for us both in this life and eternal life.

Brother Yun is a modern-day Chinese house church leader, who has suffered greatly for his faith. When he became a Christian, it was not easy to get a Bible due to state repression. He borrowed one and memorised numerous parts of the Bible, a practice he has continued through his life. He recited those words to sustain him through persecution, imprisonment, torture and beating. The more deeply we engage with the Bible, the more we make "God's word our choice", the more we encounter the permanence and depth of God's glorious love and purpose for us.

Lord, thank you for the Bible, the most precious treasure I will ever find, because it tells me of your glorious love and purpose for me.

Your word is a lamp for my feet, a light on my path.
I have taken an oath and confirmed it,
that I will follow your righteous laws.
I have suffered much;
preserve my life, Lord, according to your word.
Accept, Lord, the willing praise of my mouth,
and teach me your laws.
Though I constantly take my life in my hands,
I will not forget your law.
The wicked have set a snare for me,
but I have not strayed from your precepts.
Your statutes are my heritage forever;
they are the joy of my heart.
My heart is set on keeping your decrees to the very end.

(Psalm 119:105-112)

The word of God is the saint's portion

Lord, I have made your word my choice,
my lasting heritage;
there shall my noblest powers rejoice,
my warmest thoughts engage.

I'll read the histories of your love,
and keep your laws in sight,
while through the promises I rove,
with ever fresh delight.

In this broad land of wealth unknown,
where springs of life arise,
seeds of immortal bliss are sown,
and hidden glory lies.

The best relief that mourners have,
it makes our sorrows blessed;
our fairest hope beyond the grave,
and our eternal rest.

20. FROM ALL THAT DWELL BELOW THE SKIES

On the evening of the first Easter Day, two friends were walking back from Jerusalem to Emmaus. A stranger came alongside them and joined in with their conversation. Their faces were downcast because two days earlier Jesus had been crucified. They told the stranger: "We had hoped that he was the one who was going to redeem Israel." (Luke 24:21) Their consternation had been compounded by rumours that his body had disappeared from the tomb. The stranger was , of course, Jesus, risen from the dead, but they didn't recognise him. "He explained to them what was said in all the scriptures concerning himself." (Luke 24:27)

In 1719 Isaac published a new volume of hymns with the title "The Psalms of David, imitated in the language of the New Testament and applied to the Christian State and Worship by I.Watts." Not everyone agreed with Isaac's approach of 'Christianising' the psalms, preferring to leave interpretation to the reader of scripture. Isaac himself addressed this head on by adding some words of Jesus from Luke 24:44 to the title page: "All things must be fulfilled which were written in _ the Psalms concerning me." The psalms had been written hundreds of years before Jesus. Isaac now took it upon himself to systematically paraphrase virtually every psalm into verse form. At the same time he sought to bring out the new light shed on scripture by Jesus and the New Testament. He tackled 138 of the 150 psalms in the Bible, several broken down into multiple hymns, such as Psalm 89, from which Isaac produced 7 hymns.

He even managed to produce two alternative versions of Psalm 117, which at two verses long is the shortest psalm and the shortest chapter in the Bible. It's a good place to observe the way Isaac subtly enhances both the poetry and the message of the psalm.

Isaac introduces a distinct sense of movement. In stadium terms there's a Mexican wave going on. In the first couplet it's the creator's praise rising up from the earth towards the skies. In the second it's the redeemer's name being passed around the world from nation to nation (thus bringing into the song the coming of Jesus and the gospel for the whole world). In the fourth and final couplet the imagery is repeated but now with praise sounding from shore to shore, the movement reinforced by reference to the setting and rising of the sun.

The still point at the centre of this dance of praise is the third couplet. One of Isaac's common devices is repetition to emphasise a point. Here it's the word 'eternal' at the start of both lines. This is the solid fixed point around which the dance of creation, redemption and praise revolve and evolve. Two things stand unmoved and unchanging – our Lord's mercies and the truth of his word. The hymn benefits from its setting to the marvellous tune St.Francis (Lass tuns erfreuen), arranged by Vaughan Williams, which accentuates the sense of movement in the words and also brings in the interspersed 'alleluias' (not in Isaac's original words).

The earth turns, life hurries on. May my life revolve around the Lord's mercies and the truth of his word, and my dance of praise never cease.

Praise the Lord, all you nations;
extol him, all you peoples.
For great is his love toward us,
and the faithfulness of the Lord endures forever.
Praise the Lord.

(Psalm 117)

Praise to God from all nations

From all that dwell below the skies
let the creator's praise arise;
Alleluia! Alleluia!
Let the redeemer's name be sung
through every land, by every tongue;
Alleluia! Alleluia!

Eternal are your mercies, Lord,
eternal truth attends your word;
Alleluia! Alleluia!
Your praise shall sound from shore to shore,
till suns shall rise and set no more.
Alleluia! Alleluia!

21. BEGIN, MY TONGUE, SOME HEAVENLY THEME

Speculation was all the rage at the beginning of the Georgian era. Men bet on anything and everything. It is said that, in one London gentlemen's club, when someone fell to the ground in a stupor the members would bet on whether he was alive or dead. The government licensed lotteries in 1709. Gambling fever came to a calamitous head over a national investment scheme. Its collapse is known as the South Sea Bubble. It left many destitute and led to a number of tragic suicides. A popular song ran: "Farewell your houses, land and flocks, for all you have is now in stocks." Isaac himself spoke out against the stampede to buy South Sea stocks – also in verse:

> 'Tis said the citizens have sold
> Faith, truth and trade for South-sea gold,
> 'Tis false! For those that know can swear
> All is not gold that glistens there.

We move swiftly on to our hymn that speculates, not over stocks and shares, but about the promises of God. We may imagine Isaac sitting at his desk, a blank page before him, quill poised over the ink well, ready to begin. The first words on the page are an instruction to his own tongue – to speak, tell, sound abroad and sing this heavenly theme. As the words flow onto the page, one stands out: PROMISE.

- The promise in verse 2 is sweet, precious and beautiful grace.
- In verse 3 the promise is engraved in shining brass with text which cannot be erased.
- In verse 4 the reliability of this promise is due to its source – the one who builds the skies and

rolls the stars along. Like the speculations of his time, Isaac's theme is hopeful for the future. The difference is the security of the promise, namely the one who guarantees it.

This heavenly theme now on the page, Isaac turns from speaking *about* God to addressing his Lord directly. He recalls his opening words to his own tongue, but now asks to hear God's "heavenly tongue" speak to him. "You are mine" the Lord says, reiterating that the promises are totally grounded in God's love. This raises Isaac's song to "notes almost divine."

This hymn speaks to me as I sit with the blank page of the day ahead of me, and the blank pages of days and months and years into the future. What theme should I be writing on those blank pages? What is most important to understand and live by? Isaac tells me that the first thing on those pages should be the sweet, unshakeable, totally reliable promises of the Lord. He leaves me with one of his perfectly constructed maxims which is all about my future: "I trust the all-creating voice, and faith desires no more."

Lord, let me hear you speaking in accents clear and still. I am yours. Give me grace to trust in all your promises.

But as surely as God is faithful, our message to you is not "Yes" and "No." For the Son of God, Jesus Christ, who was preached among you by us— by me and Silas and Timothy— was not "Yes" and "No," but in him it has always been "Yes."

For no matter how many promises God has made, they are "Yes" in Christ. And so through him the "Amen" is spoken by us to the glory of God.

Now it is God who makes both us and you stand firm in Christ. He anointed us, set his seal of ownership on us, and put his Spirit in our hearts as a deposit, guaranteeing what is to come.

(2 Corinthians 1:18-22)

The faithfulness of God in his promises

Begin, my tongue, some heavenly theme,
and speak some boundless thing:
the mighty works, or mightier name
of our eternal king.

Tell of his wondrous faithfulness,
and sound his power abroad,
sing the sweet promise of his grace,
our living, active God.

Engraved, as in eternal brass,
the mighty promise shines;
nor can the powers of darkness raze
those everlasting lines.

His every word of grace is strong
as that which built the skies.
The voice that rolls the stars along
speaks all the promises.

O, might I hear your heavenly tongue
but whisper "You are mine",
those gentle words should raise my song
to notes almost divine.

How would my leaping heart rejoice,
and think my Heaven secure!
I trust the all-creating voice,
and faith desires no more.

22. I'M NOT ASHAMED TO OWN MY LORD

Francis Spufford is a prominent writer, novelist and academic. In 2013 he published a book with the tremendous title of "Unapologetic: Why, despite everything, Christianity can still make surprising emotional sense."

There's something similarly defiant and upbeat in Isaac's writing in "I'm not ashamed." He's defending the cause, standing up for two things of particular significance to him: the honour of the word of God, and the glory of the cross. Add a marching band and the old tune from Sunday School days, when all the boys stamped the wooden floor in time to these words, and you have Christianity on the front foot. Honour and glory. I'm not ashamed.

But there is, of course, a paradox in the phrase "the glory of the cross" (verse 1). The cross of Jesus was quite the opposite of glory. Crucifixion was invented by the Romans to deliver a combination of utter shame and dreadful agony. It meant suffering and humiliation. As Hebrews 12:2 says: "For the joy set before him he endured the cross, scorning its shame."

Isaac merges two cross-centred passages of scripture in this hymn, from 2 Timothy and Mark's Gospel.

Isaac's ascription is to 2 Timothy 1:12 where Paul, a man who endured much suffering, writes: "That is why I am suffering as I am. Yet this is no cause for shame." In our time and all times, there is an association between suffering and shame. It forms in our self-perception as well as in our fears of the perceptions of others. It's not good to feel ill or weak or down on your luck. It's awful to feel rejection or pain or hopelessness. The cross encapsulates all of that shame and more besides. There is no pleasantness or satisfaction in it. But Paul has moved beyond shame, in fact, his cross-shaped suffering has become a defining characteristic of his work for God's kingdom. Paul is upheld in this work because he knows who he has believed, he is convinced that he can entrust his life, his future to Jesus on whose life he has moulded his own. Isaac captures this beautifully, in a second verse that repeats the name, the name of Jesus as the only thing in which Isaac puts his trust. The third verse reiterates that what has been committed to Jesus' hands is firm and secure.

The second passage from scripture blended into this hymn is Mark 8:34-38, which contains some of the most challenging words of our Lord about our calling: "Whoever wants to be my disciple must deny themselves and take up their cross and follow me.....If anyone is ashamed of me and my words in this adulterous and sinful generation, the Son of Man will be ashamed of them when he comes in his Father's glory with the holy angels."

The final stanza echoes the first but with an important twist. Isaac began the lyrics by not being ashamed to own his Lord's name. Now, at the conclusion of the hymn it is Jesus owning Isaac's "worthless name." He is not ashamed of Isaac.

Lord, make me defiant in the face of the injustice in our world, and, by your grace working in me, make me brave enough to take up my cross and follow you.

For I am not ashamed of the gospel, because it is the power of God that brings salvation to everyone who believes: first to the Jew, then to the Gentile.

(Romans 1:16)

And of this gospel I was appointed a herald and an apostle and a teacher. That is why I am suffering as I am. Yet this is no cause for shame, because I know whom I have believed, and am convinced that he is able to guard what I have entrusted to him until that day.

(2 Timothy 1:11-12)

Not ashamed of the gospel

I'm not ashamed to own my Lord,
or to defend his cause;
maintain the honour of his word,
the glory of his cross.

Jesus, my God! I know his name,
his name is all my trust;
he will not put my soul to shame,
nor let my hope be lost.

Firm as his throne his promise stands,
and he can well secure
what I've committed to his hands
till the decisive hour.

Then will he own my worthless name
before his Father's face,
and in the new Jerusalem
appoint my soul a place.

23. MY SOUL, REPEAT HIS PRAISE

In 1939, excavations at Sutton Hoo in Suffolk revealed an undisturbed Anglo-Saxon ship burial from the early 7th century. The finds include a ship, an iconic helmet and some of the most important artefacts from that era ever discovered. They reveal a great deal about the 'dark ages'.

"My soul, repeat his praise" is a kind of lost treasure. For me it was the gem of a hymn I stumbled on as I idly played through a few tunes from the Methodist Hymn Book of 1933. Perhaps the ascription of the tune caught my eye: "Selma: Traditional Scottish melody of the Isle of Arran." It is a lovely folk-melody. Then I noticed Isaac's words, powerful and beautiful in their own right, but coupled with the tune they soar! However, both hymn and tune were dropped from subsequent Methodist hymn books and are hard to find elsewhere. It happens as progress hurries on. But for me the pleasure of finding this hymn is a bit like that of a detectorist unearthing treasure in a field.

There is also an element of finding lost treasure within the message of the hymn itself. Interestingly, in the last verse, Isaac looks forward and pictures future generations finding for themselves just how precious are God's promises of love and forgiveness. In our own lifetime the Christian message has been lost to many in our own country, meaning that significant numbers of people have no experience of the love and forgiveness of God. Without that knowledge we live in a 'dark age', but the treasure is waiting to be found when the time is right. Its value is beyond measuring, the fulfilment of our highest aspirations and the meeting of our deepest needs.

Some words and equations stand out in the middle verses, that take us into this unknown world of God's love and forgiveness:

- **Grace** is the word of verse 2, and it is defined as riches that are greater than our highest thoughts and more than sufficient to meet our deepest needs.
- **Power** is the word of verse 3, the power of forgiving love, which is greater than our sins and our guilt, which is irrevocably removed by God's forgiveness.
- **Pity** (meaning compassion) is the word of verse 4, and is like that of a 'tender' parent – God knows us inside out because he made us and also because in Jesus he became one of us.

Here are the riches of his grace. This is treasure beyond price, waiting to be found. Generations may come and go, believing or not, but this love endures and this sure promise is for all time.

Lord, thank you for your priceless gifts of forgiveness and undying love.

The Lord is compassionate and gracious, slow to anger, abounding in love. He will not always accuse, nor will he harbour his anger forever; he does not treat us as our sins deserve or repay us according to our iniquities.

For as high as the heavens are above the earth, so great is his love for those who fear him; as far as the east is from the west, so far has he removed our transgressions from us. As a father has compassion on his children, so the Lord has compassion on those who fear him; for he knows how we are formed, he remembers that we are dust.

The life of mortals is like grass, they flourish like a flower of the field; the wind blows over it and it is gone, and its place remembers it no more.

But from everlasting to everlasting the Lord's love is with those who fear him, and his righteousness with their children's children— with those who keep his covenant and remember to obey his precepts.

(Psalm 103:8-18)

For I am convinced that neither death nor life, neither angels nor demons, neither the present nor the future, nor any powers, neither height nor depth, nor anything else in all creation, will be able to separate us from the love of God that is in Christ Jesus our Lord.

(Romans 8:38-39)

Abounding Compassion of God

My soul, repeat his praise,
whose mercies are so great;
whose anger is so slow to rise,
so ready to abate.

High as the heavens are raised
above the ground we tread,
so far the riches of his grace
our highest thoughts exceed.

His power subdues our sins
with his forgiving love,
far as the east is from the west
is all our guilt removed.

The pity of the Lord
to those that fear his name,
is such as tender parents feel;
he knows our feeble frame.

Your great compassions, Lord,
to endless years endure;
and children's children ever find
your words of promise sure.

24. I GIVE IMMORTAL PRAISE

Throughout the course of the church's year God's goodness is revealed to us through stories of his mighty deeds. We start with the creation, hear of the coming of Jesus, his ministry, death and resurrection, and the coming of the Holy Spirit. When that story has unfolded over around seven months, we reach Trinity Sunday, a day to reflect on the God who is revealed through these stories as one God known in three persons. It's the height of Christian theology and the heart of Christian belief. But it's very difficult to understand. Here's how Isaac approaches it in his hymn on the Trinity, which is structured with a verse each for Father, Son and Holy Spirit, followed by a concluding verse.

His starting point is not definition or explanation. This is not putting the creed into verse. Instead, it's about worship. Each verse begins with praise, glory and worship to God, anchored by the word "immortal", recognising that these subjects require an eternal perspective.

Isaac focuses on the actions of God rather than trying to define his being or nature. The story tells of the Father's love, of sending his Son; the story of Jesus buying us with his blood, living and reigning; the story of the Holy Spirit bringing the dead sinner to life and filling the soul with joy. Our God is defined by his activity.

There are links in the verses that bind the actions of Father, Son and Holy Spirit together.
- The Father's verse introduces the death of Jesus for our sake;

- the Son's verse references the "fruit" of his pains recalling language and meaning of the fruits of the Spirit;
- and the words of the Spirit's verse refer to both the creation of the universe and the transformation of each individual person.

Isaac was criticized at one point in his life for trying too hard to justify the reasonableness of the Christian faith. His opponents claimed that this gave the primary place to reason, thus allowing reason to judge God rather than the other way around. There is no hint of this in "I give immortal praise." In fact the hymn finishes with one of Isaac's classic phrases: "Where reason fails, with all her powers, there faith prevails, and love adores."

When Isaac wrote this hymn he began it in the first person "I." Although hymn-books generally change this to "We", I've restored the "I" for our text. These are fine words for our personal devotion and our approach to the inexpressible wonder and mystery of our God.

Lord, I may not understand everything about you, but I believe and love and adore you.

Oh, the depth of the riches of the wisdom and knowledge of God! How unsearchable his judgments, and his paths beyond tracing out! Who has known the mind of the Lord? Or who has been his counselor?

Who has ever given to God, that God should repay them? For from him and through him and for him are all things. To him be the glory forever! Amen.

(Romans 11:33-36)

Song of praise to the blessed Trinity

I give immortal praise
to God the Father's love,
for all our comforts here,
and better hopes above;
he sent His own eternal Son,
to die for sins that man had done.

To God the Son belongs
immortal glory too,
who bought us with His blood
from everlasting woe:
and now He lives, and now He reigns,
and sees the fruit of all His pains.

To God the Spirit's name
immortal worship give,
whose new-creating power
makes the dead sinner live;
his work completes the great design,
and fills the soul with joy divine.

Almighty God, to you
be endless honours done,
the undivided Three,
and the mysterious One:
where reason fails, with all her powers,
there faith prevails, and love adores.

25. I'LL PRAISE MY MAKER

After a long career of faithful service, John Wesley's life was drawing to a close. He preached at City Road in London on Tuesday evening 22nd February 1791. The hymn before the sermon was "I'll praise my maker." After one final sermon at Leatherhead he was confined to his bed. When some friends visited he broke out in song with a vigour that astonished them. "I'll praise my maker", the first two verses. The next day as he drifted in and out of consciousness they heard him trying to repeat the hymn once again, but he could only say, over and over, "I'll praise...I'll praise."

John Wesley had a special affection for this hymn. It has been described as his 'favourite psalm." As early as 1737, during his short-lived stay in America, he had published it in his Charlestown collection of hymns. In doing so he made some small adaptations which have remained with the hymn ever since. He removed two verses, changed the first line from "with my breath" to "while I've breath" and in the third verse "The Lord pours eyesight on the blind" rather than "hath eyes to give the blind." I've used Wesley's changes in the text below.

Isaac's words spring from Psalm 146. Verses 2 and 3 paraphrase the psalm's marvellous description of the blessedness of those whose help is the God of Jacob and whose hope is in the Lord their God:
- wrongs are righted;
- the hungry are fed;
- prisoners are freed;
- the blind see;

- there is help for widows, orphans and strangers in distress;
- the "sinking mind" is supported;
- there is peace for the "labouring conscience"
- the Lord faithfully loves, lifts up, watches over and sustains those who rely on him.

It is not hard to recognise our needs somewhere in that list, and the ways in which the Lord has loved, supported and blessed us.

The psalm sets all of this in the time of our life on earth – "as long as I live", "all my life." This prompts Isaac to write line 1 – "I'll praise my maker while I've breath." Verses 3 and 4 of the psalm note that the plans of princes and mortal men come to nothing on the very day that they die. This gives Isaac a springboard to launch his hymn into Christian hopes of eternal life. Our unworthy thoughts, plans and activities of this life may well die with us, but the praises of God and our nobler powers will endure for ever. And with that thought this whole picture of blessedness is raised from its ancient roots to expand across the broad sweep of eternity. The blessedness does not now stop at death. Instead death brings nobler powers for praise. Isaac anticipates blessedness - praise, life, thought, being last – spanning seamlessly this life and the life to come.

Lord, I praise you now and trust you for eternity.

Praise the Lord, my soul.
I will praise the Lord all my life;
I will sing praise to my God as long as I live.

Do not put your trust in princes, in human beings, who cannot save. When their spirit departs, they return to the ground; on that very day their plans come to nothing.

Blessed are those whose help is the God of Jacob,
whose hope is in the Lord their God.

(Psalm 146:1-5)

Praise to God for his goodness and truth.

I'll praise my Maker while I've breath,
and when my voice is lost in death,
praise shall employ my nobler powers.
My days of praise shall never pass,
while life, and thought, and being last,
or immortality endures.

Happy the one whose hopes rely
on Israel's God: he made the sky,
and earth, and seas, with all their train.
His truth for ever stands secure;
he saves the oppressed, he feeds the poor,
and none shall find his promise vain.

The Lord pours eyesight on the blind;
the Lord supports the sinking mind;
he sends the labouring conscience peace;
he helps the stranger in distress,
the widow and the fatherless,
and grants the prisoner sweet release.

I'll praise him while he lends me breath;
and when my voice is lost in death,
praise shall employ my nobler powers.
My days of praise shall never pass,
while life, and thought, and being last,
or immortality endures.

26. GIVE ME THE WINGS OF FAITH TO RISE

Philip Doddridge was a friend and supporter of Isaac through his later years. Once, when leading worship in a barn, Philip followed his sermon with the hymn "Give me the wings of faith." Afterwards he wrote to Isaac to report that this gathering of ordinary country people had been so deeply affected by the words, some were in tears: "The clerk told me he could hardly utter the words of it."

It touches on a question that runs deep and affects each one of us as the years draw on. What has happened to those we love but see no longer?

Mitch Albom's beautiful story "The Five People You Meet In Heaven" follows a maintenance man called Eddie through his death (in a fairground accident) into Heaven. He is welcomed by five people in turn whose lives and deaths were, in different ways, intertwined with his life. In the different conversations, both Eddie and the people he meets find that explanation and understanding lead to reconciliation and healing.

What has happened to those we love but see no longer? Isaac prays for a glimpse into that reality beyond death, and sees the boundless joy and bright glory of the saints. Isaac is referring to saints in the broadest sense of all believers, not just those canonised by the church. These are people just like us, who have struggled through life with plenty of tears and sorrow.

Isaac imagines falling into conversation with them. What did they do to inherit 'beyond the veil' a life of joy and glory? The answer is nothing to do with service or holiness or faithful obedience or any human achievements. Their residence in this land of pure delight is all down to Jesus, whose death has given them life.

Isaac's comment is that their secret was to 'mark' Jesus' footsteps, and, their hearts inspired by him, they followed him all the way to Heaven. We are grateful to Jesus, whose footsteps were those of the incarnate God, and for those who have shown us the way by following in those same footsteps. We look forward to rising with them to the life immortal.

This hymn was a favourite of my father-in-law, Hugh. For the last few years of his life our evenings would end with a chat, a reading and a hymn or two. Very often he would want "Give me the wings of faith" to the new tune (San Rocco), which he would launch into with gusto. Many the saints he pictured as he sang Isaac's words. Hugh was a marvellous witness himself, a walker in those footsteps, and I'm looking forward to a re-union with him one day. I'll play. He can sing.

Lord, give me faith in you for the future, and give me a vision of your goodness and love that are at the very heart of the whole creation.

Therefore, since we are surrounded by such a great cloud of witnesses, let us throw off everything that hinders and the sin that so easily entangles.

And let us run with perseverance the race marked out for us, fixing our eyes on Jesus, the pioneer and perfecter of faith. For the joy set before him he endured the cross, scorning its shame, and sat down at the right hand of the throne of God.

Consider him who endured such opposition from sinners, so that you will not grow weary and lose heart.

(Hebrews 12:1-3)

The examples of Christ and the saints

Give me the wings of faith to rise
within the veil, and see
the saints above, how great their joys,
how bright their glories be.

Once they were mourners here below,
and poured out sighs and tears;
they wrestled hard, as we do now,
with sins, and doubts, and fears.

I ask them whence their victory came,
they, with united breath,
ascribe their conquest to the Lamb,
their triumph to his death.

They marked the footsteps that he trod
his zeal inspired their breast;
and, following their incarnate God,
possess the promised rest.

Our glorious leader claims our praise
for his own pattern given,
while the long cloud of witnesses
show the same path to Heaven.

27. I SING THE ALMIGHTY POWER OF GOD

It seems hard to believe today, but back in the 1970s television used to shut down each night around midnight, in some cases with a faith reflection. Richard Adams, a local teacher and preacher, wrote and presented some entertaining epilogues for Anglia TV. The plot was always basically the same: Richard would be doing something when God appeared and they would have a chat. The talks were enhanced by cartoon drawings in which God was depicted as an old man with a white beard and a white biblical robe. The talks were collected in two excellent books, "So God said to me..." and "Seen God Lately."

In "I sing the Almighty Power of God" Isaac employs a similar technique insofar as God interrupts the song half-way through. The first three verses feature Isaac busy observing the world around, then verses 4 and 5 are addressed to God, before a final verse in our direction.

So, to start with, in his mind's eye, Isaac is looking out over a glorious view. Sweeping valleys, mountain ranges, the play of light on the waves spread before him. A panoramic view of this good earth at its most majestic. And Isaac sings. He roars like the waves. His heart overflows with music. He bellows to the sky, to the sea, to the hills.

He sings of the astounding power that built mountains, unleashed oceans and constructed the sky. He sings of the order of the universe, observed and experienced in this moment, and the wisdom that made this so. The sun, the moon, the stars structure his music. The song carries his thought further, to the goodness to be seen and known in this awesomely beautiful, impeccably ordered creation. As in the first chapter of Genesis, the unfolding creation is pronounced 'good'. Isaac sees and feels all of this in an echo of what God himself saw and felt as creation was spoken into being in the very beginning.

For three exuberant verses the man is swept up in the wonder of creation. He is carried away by an experience of the power and wisdom and goodness of the Creator. He is lost in the echoes of his song across the wide open landscape stretching out before him.

Then suddenly he turns round. There beside him is God. And Isaac falls into respectful but intimate conversation with his Lord along these lines: "Wherever I look, Lord, I see your wonders, even if my eyes are fixed to the ground beneath my feet. Your glory is in the humblest plant or flower, just as it is in the most tremendous storm. All of creation flows from your power and wisdom and goodness."

Now Isaac turns once more, away from the view, away from God. Now he is looking directly at me, his listener, and speaking to me. This God, with whom Isaac has just had such a conversation, has a wonderful care for each of us. How could we ever forget him?

Lord, thank you for the wonder of creation, and for your endless love for all that you have made.

He spreads out the northern skies over empty space; he suspends the earth over nothing.
He wraps up the waters in his clouds, yet the clouds do not burst under their weight.
He covers the face of the full moon, spreading his clouds over it.
He marks out the horizon on the face of the waters for a boundary between light and darkness.

The pillars of the heavens quake, aghast at his rebuke.
By his power he churned up the sea;
    by his wisdom he cut Rahab to pieces.
By his breath the skies became fair;
    his hand pierced the gliding serpent.
And these are but the outer fringe of his works;
    how faint the whisper we hear of him!

Who then can understand the thunder of his power?

(Job 26:7-14)

Praise for creation and providence

I sing the almighty power of God,
that made the mountains rise;
that spread the flowing seas abroad,
and built the lofty skies.

I sing the wisdom that ordained
the sun to rule the day;
the moon shines full at His command,
and all the stars obey.

I sing the goodness of the Lord,
that filled the earth with food;
he formed the creatures with his word,
and then pronounced them good.

Lord, how your wonders are displayed
where'er I turn my eye,
if I survey the ground I tread,
or gaze upon the sky!

There's not a plant or flower below,
but makes your glories known;
and clouds arise and tempests blow,
by order from your throne.

His hand is my perpetual guard,
he keeps me with his eye:
why should I then forget the Lord,
who is for ever nigh?

28. JOY TO THE WORLD

If you want to feel the Christmas spirit any time of year just find the video of the massed ranks of the Mormon Tabernacle Choir and Orchestra performing "Joy to the World" at Temple Square, accompanied by the Band of the United States Air Force Reserve and an enormous concert organ. The expansive stage is decked with red flowers and foliage and twinkles with Christmas lights. If the song and the spectacle doesn't blow you away, nothing will. It's hardly surprising that, based on one survey at least, this hymn is the most popular piece of Christmas music in North America.

Isaac would probably be surprised and delighted with the effect, whether or not Christmas was in his mind when he wrote the words. Its success clearly owes much to the joyful tune, which is a perfect fit for the words. With or without orchestra, the melody starts like a run of church bells before rising again like the whole creation rising to greet the king. Then the repetition of the last line of each verse coincides with, firstly, heaven and nature singing, then, secondly, the repeating of the sounding joy, and, finally, gloriously, the wonders, the wonders of his love.

The words waited over a hundred years to be wedded to that tune. There remains an element of mystery about the origins of the music. Lowell Mason had a large part to play, publishing a version in 1836, which finally settled into its current shape in 1848 with his arrangement in "the National Psalmist." He called it "Antioch" and added that it was "arranged from Handel." Over the years the tune has been attributed to Mason, Handel or both. The first four notes are identical to "Lift Up Your Heads" in Handel's "Messiah." The third line also has some resemblance to "Comfort Ye" from the same oratorio.

Was the attribution to Handel Mason's personal homage to the great composer or embarrassment at the unintended plagiarism? Well, probably neither, because the music scholar John Wilson has found an original version of the tune set to a Wesley hymn three years earlier than Mason's first version.

But now take away the trimmings and the tune, and you will find that Isaac's words possess a depth and beauty of their own. Inspired by, rather than paraphrasing, Psalm 98, Isaac finds in the psalm a jubilant expression of the significance of Jesus' coming to earth. The psalm ends with a promise, Isaac's hymn ends with the fulfilment of that promise.

The impetus of this hymn is wonderful love. The resulting blessing to all creation is beautiful righteousness or wholeness, which spills into joy for the world. Isaac's response is this great song sounding from the whole creation, rising up to greet Jesus. He is its true and gracious king, whose coming to earth has established just such a kingdom in the hearts of those who will receive him.

Lord, may there be room in my heart for you, for your righteousness, and for the wonders of your love.

Sing to the Lord a new song,
for he has done marvellous things;
his right hand and his holy arm have worked salvation for
him.
The Lord has made his salvation known
and revealed his righteousness to the nations.
He has remembered his love and his faithfulness to Israel;
all the ends of the earth have seen the salvation of our God.

(Psalm 98:1-3)

For God so loved the world that he gave his one and only
Son, that whoever believes in him shall not perish but have
eternal life.

(words of Jesus in John 3:16)

The Messiah's Coming and Kingdom

Joy to the world, the Lord is come!
Let earth receive her King!
Let every heart prepare Him room,
and heaven and nature sing.

Joy to the earth, the Saviour reigns!
Let men their songs employ,
while fields and floods, rocks, hills, and plains
repeat the sounding joy.

He rules the world with truth and grace,
and makes the nations prove
the glories of His righteousness
and wonders of His love

29. JESUS SHALL REIGN

The year 1688 saw England's Glorious Revolution. Duke William of Orange, husband of Mary Stuart, landed with a small army at Brixham, but the couple were made King and Queen with little resistance. Mary's brother, James II, fled reluctantly to leave a vacant throne. Some historians trace the shaping of our current parliamentary democracy to this moment.

Isaac was around 13 years old. The revolution was glorious for Isaac in that it marked the end of the threat of persecution of Dissenters. He would never be imprisoned for his faith as his father was. The new regime made Isaac's subsequent career possible. There were still popular and institutional prejudices against Dissenters – such as when Isaac had to make a choice between his Dissenting faith and the opportunity to attend Oxford or Cambridge Universities. Even so, Isaac flourished under this new regime, as did science, reason, exploration and industry.

"Jesus shall reign" is about a glorious revolution and a new king. It has its origins in Psalm 72, a prayer for a king that evolves into a longing for God's chosen one (or Messiah) to bring God's reign on earth. Isaac takes that future longing and expresses it as a future promise that will one day come true in Jesus. In Jesus it becomes a worldwide, all-encompassing promise stretching from shore to shore, wherever the sun sets and rises; and it becomes cosmic, eternal promise with reference to both the sun and the moon. This is followed by a delightful verse describing the adoration and love of Jesus on that day, with praises crowning his head, and the sound of his name like sweet perfume. Endless prayer, daily worship, the promise fulfilled.

Then, in verse 4, Isaac subtly but dramatically changes tense from future to present. The reign of Jesus is a future promise, but it has also already begun. Where Jesus reigns now, blessings already abound. The glorious revolution sets prisoners free, brings rest to the weary. This is the promise coming true already, an anticipation of what is to come.

The last verse returns to the cosmic sphere as the whole of creation is brought into view. Humans, animals, insects, birds and sea creatures, trees, plants, the earth – all so often misused and exploited at the present time – are now invited by Isaac to rise. The reign of Jesus, which has already begun, brings blessings in abundance for all, and in the future will bring peace, compassion and fulfilment to all.

So let them all rise and honour him. Let us rise and honour him. We are listening to the song of the angels now. Let all the earth reply AMEN!

Lord Jesus, perfect king, reign in me.

May he rule from sea to sea and from the River to the ends of the earth. May the desert tribes bow before him and his enemies lick the dust. May the kings of Tarshish and of distant shores bring tribute to him. May the kings of Sheba and Seba present him gifts. May all kings bow down to him and all nations serve him.

For he will deliver the needy who cry out, the afflicted who have no one to help. He will take pity on the weak and the needy and save the needy from death. He will rescue them from oppression and violence, for precious is their blood in his sight.

Long may he live! May gold from Sheba be given him. May people ever pray for him and bless him all day long. May grain abound throughout the land; on the tops of the hills may it sway. May the crops flourish like Lebanon and thrive like the grass of the field. May his name endure forever; may it continue as long as the sun.

Then all nations will be blessed through him, and they will call him blessed. Praise be to the Lord God, the God of Israel, who alone does marvellous deeds. Praise be to his glorious name forever; may the whole earth be filled with his glory. Amen and Amen.

(Psalm 72:8-19)

Christ's kingdom among the Gentiles

Jesus shall reign where'er the sun
does his successive journeys run;
his kingdom stretch from shore to shore,
till moons shall wax and wane no more.

For him shall endless prayer be made,
and praises throng to crown his head;
his name like sweet perfume shall rise
with every morning sacrifice.

People and realms of every tongue
dwell on his love with sweetest song;
and infant voices shall proclaim
their early blessings on his name.

Blessings abound where'er he reigns,
the prisoner leaps to lose his chains;
the weary find eternal rest,
and all the sons of want are blessed.

Let every creature rise and bring
their special honours to our King;
angels descend with songs again,
and earth repeat the long Amen.

30. WHEN I SURVEY THE WONDROUS CROSS

In 1373 a young woman was close to death. The last rites were performed, but she recovered. During the illness she had a number of visions. She thought and prayed about these visions over the next thirty years. Her reflections are known to us as "Revelations of Divine Love." The woman is Mother Julian of Norwich. She is credited with the first book written by a woman in English. At the heart of her experience, and her book, is watching Jesus' suffering on the cross.

"When I survey the wondrous cross" is undoubtedly one of the greatest hymns ever written. It is an expression of adoration at the foot of the cross. On the day of its writing, however, Isaac's starting point is elsewhere. The Bible is open at Galatians 6:14. Here we find the concluding personal touches to a letter in which St.Paul has argued forcefully against the hankering of the Galatians for Law, laws, and their own achievements. Paul's response was: "May I never boast except in the cross of our Lord Jesus Christ. "

Isaac finds his mind's eye drawn to the cross. It lays bare the futility of the vain things in which we trust. It exposes the pride that casts a spell on us.

The prophet Elijah famously triumphed in the contest with false prophets on Mount Carmel. Despite their best efforts, the prophets of Baal were unable to conjure up fire to ignite a sacrifice. On Elijah's turn, he poured water over the sacrifice then prayed to the one true God. His prayer was answered with fire. Isaac is pouring contempt on his pride, like water dousing the sacrifice, the vain things are sacrificed "to his blood." This is the moment that Isaac's sacrifice of his vanity meets the sacrifice of Jesus' blood on the cross.

Now Isaac's eyes are lifted to the man on the cross. In another brilliant image, sorrow and love flow like blood from the broken body. Isaac invites us to share a sense of wonder as we gaze with him. Come and see the blood, the sorrow, the love. Observe a crown made of thorns but the most precious crown in human history.

Despite the intensity of this vision, Isaac has not lost his thread from Galatians 6:14. For in this moment Isaac realizes that all else in the world is meaningless in comparison with the cross. The revelation of divine love and the depth of wonderful mysteries are experienced by Isaac as he gazes on the cross. His response is an outburst of praise. He imagines possessing everything in creation, and somehow gathering it up and bringing it as a gift to Jesus. But even such a gift is an inadequate response to the amazing love of Jesus revealed on the cross.

Love so amazing, so divine, demands my soul, my life, my all.

May I never boast except in the cross of our Lord Jesus Christ, through which the world has been crucified to me, and I to the world.

(Galatians 6:14)

Crucifixion to the world by the cross of Christ

When I survey the wondrous cross
on which the prince of glory died,
my richest gain I count but loss,
and pour contempt on all my pride.

Forbid it, Lord, that I should boast,
save in the death of Christ my God:
All the vain things that charm me most,
I sacrifice them to his blood.

See from his head, his hands, his feet,
sorrow and love flow mingled down!
Did e'er such love and sorrow meet?
or thorns compose so rich a crown?

His dying crimson, like a robe,
spreads o'er his body on the tree;
Then am I dead to all the globe,
And all the globe is dead to me.

Were the whole realm of nature mine,
that were a present far too small;
love so amazing, so divine,
demands my soul, my life, my all.

REFERENCES AND FURTHER READING

Ackroyd, Peter (2016), The History of England Volume IV Revolution, London: MacMillan.

Adams, Richard (1978), So God Said To Me..., London: Epworth Press.

Adams, Richard (1978), Seen God Lately? London: Epworth Press.

Beynon, Graham (2013), Isaac Watts His Life and Thought, Fearn: Christian Focus.

Bradley, Ian (2005), The Daily Telegraph Book of Hymns, London: Continuum.

Brother Yun with Paul Hattaway (2002), The Heavenly Man, London: Monarch Books.

Gant, Andrew (2015), O Sing Unto The Lord, London: Profile Books Ltd.

Gooder, Paula (2011), Heaven, London: SPCK.

Fountain, David (1974), Isaac Watts Remembered, Harpenden: Gospel Standard Baptist Trust Ltd.

Manning, Bernard L. (1942), The Hymns of Wesley and Watts, London: Epworth Press.

Piper, John (2016), A Peculiar Glory, Wheaton, Illinois: Crossway (published in UK by Inter-Varsity Press).

Rosman, Doreen (2003), The Evolution of the English Churches 1500-2000, Cambridge: Cambridge University Press.

Telford, John (1934), the New Methodist Hymn-book Illustrated, London: Epworth Press.

Virgoe, Norma and Williamson, Tom (eds.) (1993), Religious Dissent in East Anglia, Norwich: University of East Anglia.

Watson, J.R. (2005), Awake My Soul – Reflections on Thirty Hymns, London: SPCK.

Watson, Richard and Trickett, Kenneth (eds.) (1988), Companion to Hymns & Psalms, Peterborough: Methodist Publishing House.

Walker Art Gallery, Liverpool, The Eighteenth Century

https://www.ccel.org/ccel/watts/psalmshymns.html

https://www.ccel.org/ccel/watts/divsongs.html

https://hymnary.org/

https://www.telegraph.co.uk/history/11219434/Berlin-Wall-How-the-Wall-came-down-as-it-happened-25-years-ago-live.html

https://www.bl.uk/works/robinson-crusoe

https://www.bl.uk/restoration-18th-century-literature/articles/robinson-crusoe-a-world-classic

Made in the USA
Columbia, SC
20 December 2024

50017211R00083